*Many know King David only for
his bright hour with Goliath
and his dark hour with Bathsheba;
yet the Old Testament uses
66 chapters to unfold his saga.
The New Testament mentions him
no less than 59 times,
and only God knows how many of
the psalms flowed from David's pen.*

*The human spirit resonates so
universally with the heart of David
precisely because he was a street-
level, earthy man. It is not his
gargantuan mythological
proportions but the plain profile
of his humanness that makes David
"the man for all men."*

*How will this give me the heart to
keep going?*

Read on!

Finding the Heart to Go On

LYNN ANDERSON

Here's Life Publishers

Second Printing, October 1992

Published by
HERE'S LIFE PUBLISHERS, INC.
P. O. Box 1576
San Bernardino, CA 92402-1576

Library of Congress Cataloging-in-Publication Data
Anderson, Lynn, 1936- .
    Finding the heart to go on / Lynn Anderson.
        p.   cm.
    Includes bibliographical references.
    ISBN 0-89840-309-X
    1. David, King of Israel—Sermons. 2. Churches of Christ—Sermons.
3. Sermons, American. I. Title.
BS580.D3A58   1990
252'.0663—dc20   90-21258
                                            CIP

Cover design by David Marty Design.

    Unless otherwise indicated, Scripture quotations are from *The Holy
Bible: New International Version,* © 1973, 1978, 1984 by the International Bible Society. Used by permission of Zondervan Bible Publishers.
    Scripture quotations designated KJV are from the King James Version
of the Bible.

For More Information, Write:
L.I.F.E.—P.O. Box A399, Sydney South 2000, Australia
Campus Crusade for Christ of Canada—Box 300, Vancouver, B.C., V6C 2X3, Canada
Campus Crusade for Christ—Pearl Assurance House, 4 Temple Row, Birmingham, B2 5HG, England
Lay Institute for Evangelism—P.O. Box 8786, Auckland 3, New Zealand
Campus Crusade for Christ—P.O. Box 240, Raffles City Post Office, Singapore 9117
Great Commission Movement of Nigeria—P.O. Box 500, Jos, Plateau State Nigeria, West Africa
Campus Crusade for Christ International—Arrowhead Springs, San Bernardino, CA 92414, U.S.A.

Contents

*Sheep could not report on David's performance,
so, in the face of danger, he could just as well
have fled, but he didn't—*

*David has paid his dues, and he shows the
value of three vital elements when—*

*David lost his position, his integrity, his dig-
nity, and the people who cared about him, but
he reveals a sure source of hope and comfort—*

*Three steps that will help you, as they did
David, to come back from being out of touch
with God, in a hostile land—*

*Five revealing questions David might ask you
about your career—*

*David helps us see and understand a little more
of God's awesome holiness—*

*David teaches us by his example how to react
to disappointment—*

Foreword

I went to church that Sunday more out of obligation than inspiration. I arrived late, walked in unnoticed and found a seat near the back of the auditorium. I intended to sit through the lesson and sneak out before the conclusion. As a college freshman, my interests were more in sowing wild oats than knowing God's Word. Yet that night, God's Word would be sown in my heart like never before.

The speaker was different from most preachers I'd heard. He didn't rant or scream. His tone was tender. His voice was earnest and his message was relevant. Though the decision I made that night wasn't major, it was significant—I decided to come back and hear him again.

I returned the next week, and the next, and the next. Each week I sat closer to the front until I was almost at his feet. It would be at his feet that I would sit for the next four years. The change was gradual, but noticeable. I bought a new Bible. I took notes. I bought tapes. I asked questions.

Wherever Lynn Anderson taught, I was present. I stayed in the newcomers class he led long after I became a member. I showed up at banquets and special gatherings just to hear Lynn teach. Something about the way this Canadian presented the Galilean stirred my heart.

That all began in 1973. Now it is nearly twenty years later. Much has changed in the passage of this time. Lynn is now not only my mentor but a dear friend.

7

We have traveled together in Latin America and spoken together in North America. His children now have children of their own. And what he did for me as a college student he has done for literally thousands of others.

But for all that has changed, there is one thing that has not. Lynn's message is just as moving as ever. Every Sunday finds him where I first discovered him sixteen years ago — preaching in the same church to an auditorium full of listeners. (Only five days ago I heard Lynn Anderson speak again. His words were just as convicting as they were that first Sunday.)

You are about to encounter that same relevance and clarity. If you need information on David, you've picked up the right book. If you need inspiration from David, you've picked up the right book. If you want to be stirred, motivated, challenged and changed, then your wish is about to be granted.

Lynn Anderson will present David to you as he would present a friend. His research is exhaustive and his application is practical. He knows David. On this journey from the sheep pasture to the throneroom, you'll say as I said a thousand times, "Wow! I never thought of it that way before."

You are in for a great experience. Get your pen and your coffee; find a good chair; and open your mind. This book is going to touch your heart and shape your character.

Max Lucado

Prologue

In midwinter of 1809, at a log cabin in Hardin County, Kentucky, a baby boy was born to the sub-literate Lincoln family. They called the boy Abraham. Abe Lincoln! The world at large paid little mind to this obscure but history-changing child. Far bigger attractions held global attention — it was in that year that Napoleon marched iron-shod through Austria, crushing all resistance and threatening the order of the Western world.

In the year 1020 B.C. another significant birth had gone virtually unnoticed. Few took note of a red-headed little boy, born to a poor sheepherder named Jesse, near the vague parameters where the humble village of Bethlehem dwindled into desolate pasturelands. Hebrew eyes followed a far more dramatic figure. Roadways rang with war songs of the massive, swaggering, charismatic new King Saul. Yet while Saul drifted unwittingly toward disaster, God was quietly shaping the heart of the eighth and unknown son of Jesse, who would become one of the most colorful and visible figures of history. They called him David.

King David!

This book aims to lead twentieth-century, fast-lane people to points of intersection with David. The reader, hopefully, will spot himself or herself in the wide range of emotions and experiences of this struggling man.

David's era strikingly parallels our own.

Decline, disillusionment and danger: three words of our times. *Decline*? People are living in a world with no stuffing, a society in decline – and they feel the life running out of them. *Disillusionment*? Nothing works. Nothing will change. No one means what he says. *Danger*? A globe holding itself hostage at nuclear warheads' points. We are worried sick about unemployment and so terrified of AIDS that we burn down the houses of school children. Elderly urbanites die of heat suffocation, afraid to turn on the air conditioner lest they cannot pay the bill, and afraid to open the windows lest they be robbed. How do we find the heart to go on?

Those same three conditions – decline, disillusionment and danger – also marked the times when David stepped from the pastures to the palace. *Decline*. In those days the Hebrew people were descending the lower slopes of long spiritual and social decline. Joshua and Moses were forgotten. The public conscience seemed numbed by the lust-driven religions of Canaanite neighbors. After three hundred years under an assortment of judges, pure chaos prevailed. "In those days there was no king in Israel: every man did that which was right in his own eyes" (Judges 21:25, KJV).

Decline fed *disillusionment*. Leader after leader began well and ended badly. The fans screamed for a new quarterback and got one – but Saul, "the people's choice," turned out to be a psychotic and murderous blunderer.

Decline and disillusionment were surrounded by *danger*. From the Aegean Islands, a warlike maritime people had migrated to the coastal plain of Palestine. These Philistines established five city-states, ruled by five shrewd and bloody princes. Their booming economy was capped off by a monopoly on iron and blacksmiths. Israel had only bronze and wood.

The plains trembled under thousands of thundering Philistine chariots; wheels armed with spinning swords were capable of cutting down whole Israeli divisions, like mowing grass. The Philistine infantry must have resembled mobile forests of steel as weapons flashed in the desert sun. The Israelites, on the other hand, were armed only with slings, arrows, assorted farm tools, a few knives, and instruments of bronze. In fact, at one point, in all the hosts of Israel only two warriors wielded iron swords: Saul and Jonathan (1 Samuel 13:22). Even the deadly accurate Israeli arrows could not pierce the metal Philistine armor.

Israel's hosts huddled on the hillsides in terror, watching the awesome panorama unfolding on the Philistine plain. No doubt stark panic spread across the camps of Israel, tugging at the tent flaps and tightening throats. Finally, the filthy pagan enemy massacred much of the ragtag Hebrew army and carried the sacred Ark of the Covenant, the very dwelling place of God, into the land of the Philistines.

Decline. Disillusionment. Danger. The time was right for God to intervene and to make His choice (1 Samuel 13:14). Our man David was given the nod of God—but why?

Many know King David only for his bright hour with Goliath and his dark hour with Bathsheba; yet the Old Testament uses sixty-six chapters to unfold his saga. The New Testament mentions him no less than fifty-nine times, and only God knows how many of the psalms flowed from David's pen.

Millions of birth certificates of all races bear the name David or Davita. Novels, poems, paintings and movies about David touch all continents. Fluttering over every flagpole in the independent state of Israel is the *Star of David*. And in Florence, Italy, every day, people from all over the world pay money and wait in line to see a fourteen-foot marble colossus, shaped 450 years ago by the 26-six-year-old hand of Michelangelo, depicting the spirit of *David*.

Such legendary proportions are misleading, for they balloon David larger than the flesh-and-blood reality portrayed in Scripture.

David was not a "biblical character." There are no biblical characters. The people in the pages of the Bible were ordinary human beings like you and me, who just happened to be around when the Bible was being written. David is no different. In fact, the human spirit resonates so universally with the heart of David precisely because he was a street-level, earthy man. It is not his gargantuan mythological proportions but the plain profile of his humanness that makes David "the man for all men."

How will this give me the heart to keep going?

Read on!

Acknowledgments

My name is listed as the author of this book, but in actuality the work has had multiple authors. Through the past two years as these thoughts have taken shape on paper, I have relied heavily on many people.

Where I have been able to do so, I have given each person specific credit. However, as time passed, I have forgotten where some ideas came from. Other borrowed material I have lived with so long I may well be mistaking for my own. Still other ingredients have become so integrated that for me to distinguish between borrowed and original would be as difficult as unbaking a cake.

Some who will doubtless recognize evidence of uncredited contributions will be Malaki Martin, F. B. Meyer, Rick Atchley, Roy Osborne, Charles Swindoll, Gene Edwards, John Willis, and — well, the list could go on and on. Thanks to each of you for allowing me to lean on you.

Special thanks to Joseph Shulam, my beloved friend and Hebrew brother, from whom I took copious notes as he personally tutored me and physically retraced with me the steps of King David. Those marathon days with him in Israel have permanently and richly altered my worldview.

Thanks also to the beloved elders, and the Highland Church in Abilene, Texas, in whose pulpit I first tested these ideas.

Deep gratitude to my dear friend John Michener for calling week in, week out with insights, and for blessing me with his great gift of encouragement.

Thanks also to Patsy Strader and Shirley Straker for long, patient hours of typing, and to Delno Roberts for meticulous editing. And to Michael McGaughey, who chased footnotes all over America.

Most of all, thanks to Carolyn, my best friend and unflagging cheerleader for the last thirty-three years.

And to Adonai, my heart's full gratitude.

I send these reflections off now to find some readers in the hope that, in the deepest places of their hearts, God will strike music from the sweet singer of Israel.

The LORD does not look at the things
man looks at.
Man looks at the outward appearance,
but the LORD looks at the heart.
—1 Samuel 16:7

From tending the sheep he brought him to be
the shepherd of his people Jacob,
of Israel his inheritance.
And David shepherded them
with integrity of heart;
with skillful hands he led them.
—Psalm 78:71-72

Sheep could not report on David's performance, so, in the face of danger, he could just as well have fled—but he didn't . . .

Because He Had the Heart

1 Samuel 16

---

ome months back, a news anchor-woman filed a lawsuit against a major television network. Although she was a competent professional, she was fired because she was losing her looks.

Woe to those who are ugly, dumb and broke! In our times packaging seems more important than persons. Millions place appearance ahead of integrity. We want our heroes to look the part, never mind the heart. No one will be elected to high office who does not look "senatorial" or "presidential" and televise well.

The demand is no different in business. Attractive show-biz personalities set moral standards. Pursued by political parties, business corporations, talk shows and, yes, even churches, celebrities are invited to hold forth on every subject from sex to kids to God, simply because they are visible, charismatic, or photogenic.

Even in religion: Create the image. Make the impression. The shocker is, churches also feel compelled to depend on the charisma of those who "look the part."

Behind the bright colors and upbeat tempo of this Madison-Avenue mentality lurks a vicious underside as well. Tony Campolo puts it this way, "Since failure is our unforgivable sin, we are willing to ignore all forms of deviance in people if they just achieve the success symbols which we worship."[1]

In the biblical account of King David, however, God clearly bypasses appearances and zeroes in quickly on the heart of the matter. God wants His man to "have the heart," not merely "look the part."

Samuel's Search

Please speed-reverse your time-video three thousand years. Punch the "stop" button at the tenth century B.C., and zoom in on a mountaintop outside the city now called Jerusalem. Here, from Ramah, as God was cutting Samuel's orders, the revered old prophet surveyed the chief towns of his concern.

This time the Lord sent Samuel, not in search of the people's choice, but for a man Adonai Himself was grooming. Yet the king was not to be chosen from among the public figures in a major city or from a wealthy, prestigious family.

"Bethlehem?"

"Yes, Bethlehem."

"Very well. I am on my way."

The trip from Ramah to Bethlehem left plenty of time to sort through the events which led to this pivotal day.

Doubtless Samuel pondered hearts. He felt the ache in his own heart over the indifferent hearts of his people and especially over the rapidly deteriorating heart of King Saul. What was to become of this people? Things had gone wrong for so long, what could change?

Israel had clamored for a king. They were fed up with their national image. National? Hardly. With only antiquated wooden tools and inferior bronze weapons in their hands, they looked more like an overgrown band of nomads in their crude towns. So they wanted to be a respectable state—to look the part.

They had gotten their king all right, and he really looked the part. Saul stood taller than anyone around. He was humble, too, and the Holy Spirit came upon him. Yet Saul's heart had gone ugly as quickly as desert skies spoiled by a summer thunderstorm.

Samuel had served notice to Saul that God already had picked Saul's successor. The new candidate would not just "look the part"; he would have the "heart" after God's own heart. Did I see a tear roll down your cheek again, Samuel?

"Tears? Ah, yes. Saul, my Saul, didn't really want Adonai. 'The Lord *your* God' is what Saul called Adonai."

Saul! The people's choice! The one who looked the part! National nemesis. Defensively ambitious. Insecure. Psychotic. Murderous. Pain to the heart of Samuel. Affront to the name of Yahweh.

Arriving at Bethlehem, Samuel soared in spirit when he first laid eyes on Eliab, Jesse's eldest. "Here is our new king," Samuel felt. He so looked the part. Tall. Strong. Confident. Like Saul!

"No. Not like Saul."

Adonai abruptly corrected Samuel's course. "Don't be impressed by his looks. By now, Samuel, you should know this is not the way I select kings. I am not interested in the impression he will make. I want to know what is in his *heart*" (see 1 Samuel 16:7).

"Next, please."

The Youngest

Samuel quickly culled the first seven sons. Were there any more boys?

Awkwardness. Embarrassment.

"Yes. There is another boy, the youngest."

For the ancient Hebrews, "youngest" meant not only the fewest in years, but also the lowest in rank.

"He is with the sheep," blurted Jesse.

Now the poor man was forced to reveal his poverty. Rich men's sheep were kept by servants, poor men's sheep by sons. Why was this job dumped on David? Was he unplanned? Unwanted? Illegitimate? After all, there were not too many red-headed boys in Bethlehem. Or were the brothers and Jesse embarrassed because David preferred solitude, played his harp, and wrote poetry? Doing servant work? Looked down on by his family? Could this be where a line in one of David's songs came from?

> Though my father and my mother forsake me,
> The LORD will receive me (Psalm 27:10).

Whatever the reasons, Jesse's youngest son appears to have been shoved to the margins of the family. He had not been invited to the party.

What happened next surprised everyone, especially the young shepherd, sweating in the back forty. This scene spreads colorfully across the imagination.

"Who is that running toward me on the horizon? Am I dreaming? Did someone call me?"

"David! Some sort of party. The old prophet Samuel wants you to come. Won't sit down till you do!"

The Next King

David arrived, stunned and quivering. The sad-eyed old prophet wordlessly opened a horn of oil, stepped to the smelly young shepherd and, to the bewilderment of all present, poured sweet-smelling fragrance on David's head till it darkened his red beard. Just as wordlessly, the terrifying old prophet wheeled and stalked away. A voice inaudibly whispered into

David's ear, "You are to be the next king!" From that day on, the spirit of Adonai came upon David.

What encouragement to ordinary people like me! I don't need to look like Tom Selleck or Cybill Shepherd to be a person. My heart is what counts! An unnamed, rejected son of a poor country sheepherder was chosen king. He was given the opportunity to become court harpist for the centuries, universally known warrior, poet laureate of history, mentor for mankind, and shadow picture of the Messiah Himself. Why? Because he was supernatural? Because he was beautiful, or talented, or tall? No. David was chosen because of *his heart!*

God will smile on us — any of us — if we just have the heart for it.

Learning the Heart

God doesn't panic and pull His leaders green. Neither does a shepherd's heart grow regal overnight. After David's selection, Saul clung to his teetering throne for forty years. During this time the Almighty was patiently grooming David's heart.

What happened in the pasture which further shaped David's heart for the palace?

"He is with the sheep," admitted Jesse.

"Where I wanted him," breathed Adonai.

David spent years in loneliness, and in the solitude he became sensitive to the things of God.

> He chose David his servant
>   and took him from the sheep pens;
>   from tending the sheep he brought him

to be the shepherd of his people
(Psalm 78:70,71).

For young David, God became both companion and audience. God wants to be ours, too, although He is often unable to get our attention because of our feverishly maintained noise levels. Flip on the TV. Turn up the stereo. Snap on the Walkman. Wind up the RPMs. As a result there remain no quiet places in our heads for reflective thoughts, and we are too distracted to hear the still, small voice. We crave noise. "We need it," we say, "to kill the boredom."

My father used to say that boredom was good for kids. Dad meant that solitude and silence multiplied by time cultivate our powers of imagination. Space between the distractions allows us to ponder the massive, quiet realities around us. When I was a kid, we lived twelve dirt-road miles from town and a mile from neighbors, and we couldn't afford noise gadgets. So, many Saturdays and warm summer afternoons, to "kill boredom," I would pace endlessly over our ranch or find a quiet place in the bushes to sit and imagine. I wrote poems and songs, invented machines, created novels, and amassed fortunes all in my imagination.

Those early experiences left me with a bent toward abstract thought and an infatuation with words. In those quiet days, alone, I fell in love with storytelling. Even today, much of the imagery through which I communicate was born in that boredom long ago. My father was right!

Best of all, there was time for my mind to wander through the universe and explore thoughts about God. In early childhood this became my habit. To a tiny degree I identify with the things the Almighty was doing in David through his loneliness.

In the quiet pasture, David sensed the natural rhythms. He emotionally photographed the pastoral shapes, colors, aromas and sounds which would be his poetic signature for all time. The pastoral solitude and silence expanded David's God-consciousness. Adonai became the heart of David's dreams, the audience to which he would always play out his role, and the Father to whom he would look first for approval or criticism.

Writing Psalms

David's pen recorded the heart music of those days. He wrote and sang his yearnings and reflections about Adonai. Thus his psalms were born. Three thousand years later, through those psalms we may enter quickly into the secret places of David's soul and on into the presence of God. David sang:

> When I consider the heavens,
>   the work of thy fingers . . .(Psalm 8:3)

and

> The heavens declare the glory of God
>   (Psalm 19:1)

and

> The voice of the LORD twists the oaks
>   and strips the forest bare (Psalm 29:9).

He also wrote of Adonai shepherding him through lush pastures and by limpid pools. The psalms are the busy roadways between the Almighty and the impressions of the shepherd's lonely heart, winding through the familiar scenes of his solitude.

Have you ever written anything like a psalm? Few people have these days. There is so little reflection and creation in a world constantly reverberating with internal noises. No exalted vision emerges from the heavens when our consciousness is a constant blur of color and motion.

Occasionally we meet genuinely reflective people, however, and we are drawn to them. They have about them a glow from the throne room. We envy them. They inspire us, convict us, soothe us. Such hearts God uses best—hearts grown sensitive to the things of God through loneliness.

As Henri Nouwen reflects:

In solitude I get rid of my scaffolding: no friends to talk with, no telephone calls to make, no meetings to attend, no music to entertain, no books to distract . . .

Solitude molds self-righteous people into gentle, caring, forgiving persons who are so deeply convinced of their own great sinfulness and so fully aware of God's even greater mercy that their life itself becomes ministry.[2]

The State of a Servant

Not only did David spend a lot of time by himself, he also clearly was lowest in the family pecking order. His brothers seemed in the habit of putting him down hard. "You don't belong in a man's world. You rate only a 'few' sheep" (see 1 Samuel 17:28). Even David's father scarcely seemed to consider David one of his sons, hiding him from Samuel.

David's work put him down, too. Shepherding was hardly designed to lend prestige. He was forced to do this dirty work gratis, his status lower even than a servant. Sheep supply no ego food, either. They never applaud their shepherds, and they don't cooperate. So the sheep range was excellent humility training.

When the hot sun of reality beat down on Saul, his heart hardened like clay. When it beat down on David, his heart melted like butter. In his humble years with the sheep, David became teachable. He frequently said things like, "Give me understanding, and I will keep your law and obey it with all my heart" (Psalm 119:34). No one is more clearly destined to excellence than a person who is hungry to learn from all comers — who humbly listens. On the other hand, no one is more likely to fail than a know-it-all.

Since God was David's only audience in the hills, David could have gotten by with neglectful mediocrity. A self-consumed person may have been satisfied just to get by. A man insensitive to the presence of God might opt for that low road, but for David, God was constant companion and observer. So he opted for excellence. Receiving no promotions or perks in the long months with the stinking sheep, David developed habits of servanthood. Expecting no strokes, he served. From the sheep pens, God chose David to be His servant (Psalm 78:70).

Developing Character

David's way cannot be bypassed on the road to character building and excellence. Opportunists attempt shortcuts by personal charisma, connections in high places, and "looking the part." Some even appear to win that way, but the rewards are superficial and short-lived. Life's most valuable character traits develop only during time at the bottom of the totem pole.

When God looked at David's heart, He saw *reverence* and *humility*. He also saw *integrity*. "David shepherded [his people] with integrity of heart" (Psalm 78:71,72).

Life in the Judean hills was hazardous on every hand. Fierce animals prowled the lonely, treacherous trails. When bears and lions threatened Jesse's meager flock, David confronted them with steely courage.

Doubtless, hard work toned David's muscles. By consistently choosing to meet all hazards head-on, David conditioned his integrity as well; courage was drilled into David's heart by repeated confrontation with hostile elements, and his integrity was shaped by long years of hard choices. Sheep could not turn in battle reports on David's performances, so, when danger threatened, he might just as easily have fled—his father would have been none the wiser—but David's integrity made him stay and fight.

Integrity is that wholeness, that genuineness, which can best be measured by what one does in a clinch when no one else will know—except God. Then is when the genuineness of our hearts is tested.

Ruth Harms Calkin defined integrity well:

You know, Lord, how I serve You
With great emotional fervor
In the limelight.
You know how eagerly I speak for You
At a women's club;
You know how I effervesce when I promote

A fellowship group.
You know my genuine enthusiasm
At a Bible study.

But how would I react, I wonder,
If You pointed to a basin of water
And asked me to wash the callused feet
Of a bent and wrinkled old woman
Day after day,
Month after month,
In a room where nobody saw
And nobody knew?[3]

In the absolute anonymity of the sheep pasture, when no one saw and no one would know, David repeatedly risked his very life for a few stinking, stubborn sheep, who could give him no personal rewards. But God was still his audience and David's own heart was supervising him. That is why he wrote:

Search me, O God, and know my heart;
    test me and know my anxious thoughts.
See if there is any offensive way in me
                        (Psalm 139:23,24).

A Desperate Need

After the disillusionment in Israel and the schizophrenic, jealous arrogance of Saul, the Hebrews desperately needed a man with the heart of David to give them the heart to go on. I need it, too. Don't you?

Disneyland was a blast the first few times through. I especially liked the Pirates of the Caribbean. The illusions of the ride were so real that when I emerged from the watery tunnel, reality seemed fake. That was the first time or two. The new then wore off and I began to spot the mechanisms which moved the animated characters. Then Disneyland became disillusionland.

So it is with our world. People are cynical. They have spotted the gizmos behind the facades. They are wise to the duplicity of the government leaders, televangelists and Madison Avenue. Trust is draining away, and hope. Most folks I know desperately need to meet a few more people who are genuinely honest, straightshooters all the way to the core. Schools need straightshooters. Business needs them, too. So do governments and churches. Most of all, our kids need to see integrity in us!

St. Francis prayed: "Most high and glorious God, bring light to the darkness of my heart. Give me right faith, certain hope and perfect charity."

Amen, Francis. Me too. Small wonder God was looking on the heart! Or that He still does!

So here we have it — at least three specific things attracted the eye of Yahweh to the heart of David: *Sensitivity. Humility. Integrity.* And all of these are born in the quiet loneliness. Each begins with faithfulness in the little things, in obscure and dangerous places, with no applause and no one to report successes. All greatness is born in such a crucible and develops gradually, over the long haul. No shortcuts. No exceptions.

My friend Rick Atchley tells a story about the great American scientist, early black educator, and founder of Tuskegee Institute, George Washington Carver, who understood the road to integrity. One day Carver said, "Lord, tell me about the universe."

The Lord said, "Now George, that's just too big for you. Why don't you let Me take care of the universe?"

So George said, "Well, Lord, then how about a peanut?"

And the Lord said, "That's about your size. You study the peanut, and I'll help you." Before Professor Carver was through, he found more than three hundred peanut products to help mankind.

How would you like to spend your entire life studying a peanut? Yet faithfulness in the peanut patch or in the pasture is indispensable in shaping a man for a palace—a man who attracts the eye of the Lord.

In God's eyes David was the best boy in Israel.

Saul looked the part—David had the heart. Every person is potentially either a David or a Saul. It is never too late or too early to make the choice.

When you aspire to greater things
Remember:
Faithfulness to God in the present allows
Him to shape your heart for the future .

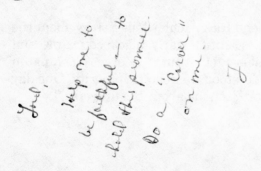

*All those gathered here
will know that it is not by sword or spear
that the LORD saves;
for the battle is the LORD's,
and He will give all of you
into our hands.*
—*1 Samuel 17:47*

*David has paid his dues, and he shows
the value of three vital elements when . . .*

Facing Giants

1 Samuel 17

rchards bloom in the friendly Judean valley where we sat on a sunny day in June 1986. Under the shade of a spreading tree, we opened *The Book* and read together about the dramatic events which occurred on this spot some three thousand years ago.

To our left rose the hill of Socoh, once crusted with shining steel—the armies of Philistia. On our right towered the hill of Azekah, once darkened with the intimidated hosts of Israel. Between these hills lies the valley of Elah, the " Valley of Blood." Through the floor of the valley winds the very stream from which David chose his five smooth stones.

As I write these words, on my desk at the feet of a miniature of Michelangelo's famous statue of David lie five stones I collected from the brook that day.

For Goliath, the forty-first morning at the valley of Elah doubtless dawned like any other day. He was a soldier, doing military things.

However, for David, the morning was unique. He rose, excited that he would journey to visit his brothers on the battlefield.

The trip to the tent of Saul placed David in double danger. The secret which Samuel had brought to the house of Jesse could not have been kept very long. The whisper from Bethlehem would almost surely have reached the ears of Saul, triggering schemes of violent jealousy.

But God planned to use David's naiveté.

Battle Positions

The stage was set: "A champion named Goliath, who was from Gath, came out of the Philistine camp. He was over nine feet tall" (1 Samuel 17:4). Goliath wore a massive helmet, a huge suit of bronze armor, and great bronze shin guards, and he had a bronze javelin slung on his back. He carried a spear with an iron point that weighed nine pounds. Before him strutted another soldier, carrying Goliath's shield.

Troops in those days were usually farmboys and shepherds conscripted into the ranks, behind a few military professionals. Frequently, in battle, each side would send a professional down to fight. Thus, a "war" could conceivably be only a representative battle between two men — in fact, it was normally so. Goliath was an abnormally big "representative" for the Philistines! This fellow was a one-man army, two feet taller than Larry Byrd or Magic Johnson. No soldier in Israel could match him.

David arrived on the scene just as the troops filed out from camp to line up for the day. The army was "going out to its battle positions, shouting the war-cry" (verse 20). For six weeks both sides had eased down the hillsides daily, strutting back and forth and shouting threats across the valley, boasting about how they would feed each other's carcasses to the birds.

Possibly this blustery standoff resembled one I once carried on with John Bailey. John is as loyal a friend as I have in the world now, but back in high school we were mortal enemies. We competed in the same sports, dated the same girls, and ran for the same offices. I did some strutting, but the fact is I was not about to get into a fistfight with John Bailey. He was tough, fast and smart—but he wasn't about to take the first swing either. He wasn't afraid of me, but should anything go wrong, being whipped by a runt would have been too embarrassing for him. So we both strutted and threatened like Israel and Philistia, and in the strutting game, the little guy has the psychological advantage.

Remember the Philistines controlled all the iron. They wore the good armor. They drove the chariot wheels armed with whirling swords, which could slice the enemy infantry to bits. They controlled the plains where chariot wheels could roll.

The Israelites, on the other hand, swung only a few iron swords and rolled no chariots, but they held the hills. To drive an iron-shod chariot up into the rocks and canyons of the Israelite heartland was virtually impossible. Also, Israel could roll rocks down from their hilltop strongholds onto the heads of the attackers. So the Philistines strutted in the valley and the Israelites strutted on the hills in a deadlocked display of bravado.

David's Intense Reaction

David was both astonished and appalled. Where is your reverence? Where is your faith? Where is your outrage?

King Saul offered huge incentives for someone to fight Goliath: wealth, reduced taxes and "my daughter to wife" (see verse 25).

Still, Saul got no takers. Why was he trying to hire someone to tackle Goliath anyway? Saul himself was the logical challenger. Aside from Goliath, he stood taller than any other man at the battle!

For David, this confrontation symbolized the cosmic struggle between good and evil, between God and idols. He could not tolerate ridicule of almighty God. "I'll fight Goliath," David finally shouted.

He held an awesome regard for holiness, nurtured in the loneliness of the sheepfold as he prayed his prayers, played his harp, and wrote his songs. In the solitude, as David dealt with utter adversity by himself, God became the central audience for his life and remained so forever. Years later, as Saul hunted David down to liquidate him, David repeatedly had opportunity to kill Saul, but would refuse to do so because Saul was "God's anointed one." David's high and holy regard for Yahweh would one day send him dancing into the city of Jerusalem because the presence of God was coming to rest in the city of God.

David was the man who, to the very end, would plead with all to place God first in their lives even after he had publicly made a shambles of his own. David would keep coming back to a holy God. So on this pivotal day in the valley of Elah, David could not bear to see the Holy Name of Yahweh spoken as a pagan expletive.

Saul chided David, "You are only a boy."

David responded, "The same God who delivered me from the lion and the bear will deliver me today" (1 Samuel 17:34-37).

Saul's answer was glib and reprehensible. "Go, and the LORD be with you."

Oh, Saul. Better the Philistines say these words than you. If you are so confident God will go with David, why don't you take God along and go out there yourself? "God go with you." Indeed!

Saul's "Help"

Saul then offered David his equipment. Knowing David could not wield the oversized armor, did Saul think, *This is a clean way to eliminate the boy who threatens my throne. Everyone will admire David for such courage — and I'll forever be rid of him?* Maybe.

Or was Saul like so many of us who repeatedly try our old ways of doing good things, only to find that our ways don't work, so we give up? Then, when someone else comes along who is willing to try a fresh approach, do we bind our old, useless ways on them?

David stumbled around, scarcely able to drag Saul's oversize armor. He didn't even know how to put it on correctly. Finally he said, "Let me use my own equipment" (verse 39).

So the drama unfolds. David walked to the brook, bent down and selected five shapely stones, and dropped them into his purse. He needed only one stone to do the job — but Goliath had four brothers!

When David stood up, one stone slid into the sling. The leather pocket slowly swung into its orbit, till it was invisible and could be traced only by the whiz, and then — whang!

Goliath never knew what hit him.

David had not approached this challenge in ignorance. No, he had grown up hearing battle legends. Surely he had looked down from the hilltops onto hundreds of acres of lethally honed and sharpened Philistine steel. David knew the terrifying facts.

Nor was David buoyed up by a mere positive mental attitude. This story has been circulated through civic clubs and sales seminars caricaturing David as the "King of Positive Mental Attitude." PMA is not what shook the valley of Elah. David went to face Goliath with genuine courage, based on three realities.

Requisite #1: Training

The first reality undergirding David's courage was his *training*.

Ranks of Israel, heirs of long Philistine intimidation, were conditioned to fear Goliath. They displayed no faith in God. Not David. He was trained in courage. He had no prior military training, but this was not the first time his hand had swung a sling. Nor was it the first time David faced a terrifying opponent. He had not waited passively for that one moment in the sun when he would jump up and seize the brass ring.

He had carefully taken advantage of his training, each step along the way.

Rick Atchley says, "Sometimes I am really troubled when people glibly say, 'Sure enjoyed your sermon, preacher. You have such a gift.' All the while, I'm thinking, *Gift? If so, it takes me thirty hours a week to unwrap it!*"

We are often inclined to attribute unusual skills, or spiritual courage like David's, to a special, brilliant gift. No, David did his quiet work back in the fold, readying himself for this moment on the field.

By the way, next time you read a good book, somewhere midway, stop. Stop and remember how many lonely, grueling hours someone put in to provide that delightful reading for you.

David had paid his dues. Besides, Goliath was not nearly so dangerous as bears and lions. When I was a child, my brother-in-law Dean Hotchkiss was treed by an angry black bear whose cub he had shot. He spent the entire night in the tree. The bear ripped up stumps and broke limbs. Once, when the bear climbed so close it looked like the certain end, Dean pulled his hatchet and made a feeble swing. The she-bear cuffed the hatchet so hard, she broke the handle and sent the head flying into the bushes. The dogs tried to run her off, but she mortally wounded them. Bears are fearsome creatures. Even seasoned hunters feel the hairs rise on their necks when they suddenly cut the fresh track of a huge grizzly.

Lions are all the more terrifying. If I had the choice to come against a nine-foot man bare-handed, or empty-handed against a lion or a bear, I would choose the man any day. David had already met the lion. And the bear. And he had killed them because he knew how. "And," he said, "God was with me."

Requisite #2: Tools

In addition to having been trained, David knew his tools. He trusted his equipment, part of which was his *natural ability*.

> Ruddy [red-haired], with a fine appearance
> [some translations say "beautiful eyes"] and
> handsome features . . . [he] knows how to play
> the harp. He is a brave man and a . . . fine-
> looking man. And the LORD is with him
> (1 Samuel 16:12,18).

What an awesome guy! Later sketches of David's "mighty men" reveal that the central three of them would terrify three hundred others, yet all three of them were terrified of David. David was no sniveling wimp.

David also trusted his *weapon* — he carried a sling. You might object, "But Goliath was a walking tank, with sword, spear, armor bearer and shield. And the guy was nine feet tall! A sling?"

Never underestimate the sling. We may be put off by images of a child's limb-crotch and rubber-band slingshot, but this is not what David carried into battle. His weapon was mobile, a decided advantage over the heavy and cumbersome paraphernalia of Goliath, for which the Philistine even needed an assistant, an armor bearer. In contrast to Goliath's heavy trappings, the sling weighed only ounces. David could carry it easily wherever he wished and could whip it out in a flash and be ready for combat.

The accuracy of slings is incredible. Roy Osborne, a friend of mine, tells of watching a young man
sitting under a Palestinian shade tree herding goats by
whizzing rocks, using his sling with pinpoint accuracy.
The boy would sail a missile in front of each stray's
nose, hazing him back to the flock. Even today, some
middle-Eastern sling-masters can kill a pigeon in flight.
No wonder David's stone pierced Goliath's helmet and
found the giant's forehead!

In addition to mobility and accuracy, a sling
has awesome power, another advantage for David. My
friend asked the young Palestinian boy to see if he could
hit a fig tree some sixty yards away. He fired a small
stone which not only struck the tree dead center, but
with such velocity that the missile also burrowed
through the bark, more than an inch into the trunk.
While the range of a spear was only the distance a
strong arm could throw it, a sling was lethal at distances
of well over a hundred yards. So actually, Goliath didn't
stand a chance, armed with his stubby and unweildy
hand-to-hand combat weapons while David was armed
with the ancient equivalent of a high-powered rifle.

David was confident because he knew his
tools—but he did not know Saul's tools. Another's
weapons always drain our courage. Frequently, some
Christian will develop a weapon for spiritual warfare,
such as a devotional technique, which is extremely
meaningful in his own life. Then he will franchise it and
attempt to bind his weapons on another brother's back.
Cultish sects have done this for centuries.

Take a lesson from David, the man who used
his own weapon.

Requisite #3: Trust

Training and tools were not the sum of David's courage, however. Many other trained Israeli soldiers carried slings to the valley of Elah, but none had used them because they all lacked trust in God.

Training. Tools. Trust. These three undergirded David's courage, but trust was the major factor which set his courage apart from that of the others. His heart was fixed on God. "The LORD," claimed David, "who delivered me from the paw of the lion and the paw of the bear will deliver me from the hand of this Philistine" (1 Samuel 17:37).

David regularly communed with God. He knew his God (unlike some of his Israeli brothers who may have feared Dagon of Philistia more than they trusted Yahweh). David knew Yahweh, the God of power.

> To you, O LORD, I lift up my soul,
>   in you I trust, O my God.
> Do not let me be put to shame,
>   nor let my enemies triumph over me
>   (Psalm 25:1,2).

Negative Effects of Pessimism

One of the most ungodly attitudes possible is pessimism—negativism which constantly says "it can't be done." People sin this way. So do churches.

One of the elders of our church asked me a few days ago, "What are your thoughts on our building expansion plans considering the deep economic recession we are experiencing?"

My negative response was, "Man, I'd be un-easy in our economic climate."

He replied, "Well, I've done some historical research. Let's see. Our first building was started in 1929. What do you know about the economy in 1929? The second expansion project was launched in 1937." I remembered that my father only recently finished pay-ing off the debts he incurred during the depression of the 1930s.

"Do you realize," pressed the elder, "that every one of our last five building expansions began smack in the middle of an economic depression?"

Thank God for this elder's faith. He would not allow circumstances to make him think negatively — but my pessimism had nearly killed progress.

However, the worst pessimism is not usually over something as mundane and concrete as building expansion. The larger, more cursed pessimism plaguing some believers is that they really don't believe people change. They doubt that relationships can be restored, habits broken, marriages saved, adolescents turned around. Are people locked in? An ugly, faithless pes-simism often sends folks into circles, wringing their hands, expecting nothing significant to happen, and mumbling, "Ain't it awful!"

Hear this: If you are a vibrant Christian, you believe in the power of God to change people in this old world. Change is the name of the game. David's trust lay in Yahweh! Not in Dagon of the Philistines who breaks when he falls because he is made of stone. David trusted . . .

the God who made the world and everything in
it [who] does not live in temples built by hands
. . . [rather] he himself gives all men life and
breath and everything else (Acts 17:24,25).

Every time we draw a breath, God is at work
in our bodies. David spoke not about *a* living God but
about *the* living God—the only one there is, the God of
heaven and earth. Armed with such trust, David went
out and, hurling a little stone found in a brook in the
valley of Elah, he changed the world!

Contagious Courage

Not only was David's act *courageous*, it was
also *contagious*. The giant fell. The Philistine armies
cut out and ran down the Shaaraim road.

As the Philistine bravado melted, momentum
shifted. Israel rallied in hot pursuit. Can you hear them
all screaming, "I want to kill me a giant, too"? Actually,
they could have been doing this all along—they had the
tools—but they lacked the needed courage. Now it
spread through the ranks. Courage is always contagious. One lone model of courage can remove the ex-
cuses of a whole timid nation and dispel its fear. Ghandi.
Churchill. Martin Luther King. Jesus.

Some trust equipment; others rely on personalities, buildings, computers, money—as if God's
work cannot be done without them. David trusted his
equipment, but that was not the source of his confidence. Some trust in experience to do God's work in
the world, or in tradition, education or credentials. In
fact, second-generation flagship enterprises often come
to grief on such rocks of pride. David was clearly inex-
perienced; his courage did not issue from experience.

Still others trust in trust: naive believism. Students have been known, in the flush of gullible faith, to neglect their studies, trusting in God for their grades. Some students in the university near us chose not to study for an exam because "God did not wake them in time." Their professor told them God gave them *F*'s!

Some people neglect the God-given medical profession in attempts to be healed without medicine: "Jesus will heal us." Maybe so. He has the power. But He is not obligated to do so while we ignore realities. This is not the meaning of trust. Some build edifices or ministries without counting the cost, believing that, since they have decided their project is of God, they can, by faith, obligate God to finance it.

David struck the crucial balance between tools, training and trust. Tools and training without trust equal pride. Naive trust without counting costs in terms of tools and training equals presumption. On the other hand, tools, training and trust balanced combine to produce contagious courage; they help us find the heart to go on.

When you face an overwhelming challenge
and you need contagious courage . . .
Remember:
your confidence can be based on
a well-developed balance of
training, tools and trust in God.

Saul tried to pin him to the wall
with his spear,
but David eluded him
as Saul drove the spear into the wall.
That night David made good his escape.
—1 Samuel 19:10

David left Gath and escaped
to the cave of Adullam.
—1 Samuel 22:1

THREE

*David lost his position, his integrity, his dignity,
and the people who cared about him—but he
reveals a sure source of hope and comfort . . .*

When You Hit Rock Bottom

1 Samuel 19–23

 he clang of the telephone ripped through the covers just moments after I had gotten to sleep. Harvey was waiting for me at a restaurant. He had already downed a lethal overdose and would likely be unconscious by the time I could get to him. Although he expected to be dead by the time we reached the hospital, he wanted me to take him there so that his loved ones would think he died of a coronary.

I went. He died.

Only hours before, Harvey had participated in a Bible study at our house. While his life was a maze of horrendous problems, he had not sounded suicidal. He did, however, tell the group he felt trapped, at the end of his rope, in a cave.

What does one do when trapped, at the end of the rope and in a cave? Not everyone will sink as low as Harvey — but all of us will occasionally do time in a cave.

David, too, wound up in a cave, and for clear reasons. There are many ways to cave in. Could you be in a cave of depression for similar reasons? Stripped of a job, of finances, or health, or position? Maybe the loss of a mate? Or has a trusted friend turned against you? Are you wondering if you can go on?

Security Blankets

Possibly you can identify with David, as one by one his security blankets were stripped away on his way to rock bottom. What does one do when security is stripped away? When life caves in?

David's stripping began when the sensational defeat of Goliath catapulted him from the back pasture to the front page. Then his popularity continued to skyrocket. Great for David, except his success triggered a pathological jealousy in Saul. He sent David to remote areas with a small company of men, hoping David would not return. The plan backfired. David's success only further inflated his reputation.

Saul married his daughter Michal to David for a dowry of one hundred foreskins of slain Philistines. Saul thought surely the Philistines would liquidate

David—but David came back with two hundred Philistine foreskins, doubling the dowry, and his fame as well.

Finally, Saul got personal. Three times he hurled his spear at David. Though the lances missed, David got the point and fled from his prestigious position into the fields. How fickle is fame and how disastrous the fall.

To this point in life, David had been accustomed to killing all of his problems. Bears and lions . . . giants . . . David killed them. When enemy regiments threatened his king's capital, he killed them. Now, for the first time in his life, David had to run.

David lost his position. His security began to dissolve. This was tough enough, but worse still, he began to lose the *people* he had leaned on.

People are God's gifts to us leaners. Yet, fundamental to the nature of the universe, no person can completely fulfill another person's need. Our need is too great. Persons are not God. Besides, all people will eventually leave us, because people don't last forever. One by one, David lost the people most precious to him.

First, he lost his wife. Michal loved David, so Saul tried to get to David through her. He sent murderers to David's house to kill him in the night, but Michal smuggled him out through a window and covered for him till he could escape. That's when David lost her. He and Michal would be together again, years later, but things would never be the same. Michal's heart would not beat with David's heart, and a faith gap would yawn between them the rest of their days.

People lose mates. Mates leave; they die. Divorce separates and leaves grief more cruel than vacancy by death. Others, like David, find themselves spiritually single. Alone in their faith, even resisted by their mates, they do not find the marriage partner someone to lean on.

Mentors

After David lost Michal, he fled to Samuel, the old prophet. Samuel had been a respected mentor, a pillar of strength in David's world. Surely David would be safe here. Saul would never touch a prophet.

Don't kid yourself, David. Saul pursued Samuel, too. Again David escaped and fled. David would not lay eyes on his revered mentor again. Even when Samuel died, David was not free to attend the funeral. Another security blanket was gone.

Most men have mentors. Maybe most women do, too. The young medical student admires a physician. A young attorney needs to copy an old lawyer. Young preachers follow older preachers around. Such is important to healthy development. But we lose our mentors. We discover their feet of clay or they die or we move away from them. Even more painful, we outgrow them.

Two mentors to whom I looked as a young man were Charles Coil and Wesley Jones. I plied them with questions. I copied their lives. They both loved me like a son. Then the time came when I would ask them questions to which their answers were no better than mine. This threw me into a grief process, a time when I lost the naive wonder of my young spiritual manhood. Profound sadness surrounds the loss of a mentor. Although these men are still my friends, they are no longer my mentors.

David and Jonathan

When David lost his mentor, he fled to his friend Jonathan, the most cherished person in his life. From their first meeting, David and Jonathan grew in unity of spirit. Jonathan gave David his own bow, tunic and robe, and his sword and belt to seal their friendship. They shared the blood and glory of the battlefield. Later David would write:

> *. . . Jonathan, my brother;*
> *you were very dear to me.*
> *Your love for me was wonderful,*
> *more wonderful than that of women*
> *(2 Samuel 1:26).*

For a time Jonathan refused to believe his own father was trying to kill David. When Saul learned Jonathan was protecting David, Saul seized his spear in blind rage and attempted to murder his own son. Then David and Jonathan were forced to part.

The intense drama of their final separation was played out in an open field. David bowed three times before Jonathan, face in the dirt. They kissed each other, each soaking the other's shoulders with tears. In the end, David's grief ran the deeper — Jonathan could not forsake his father. So David was left alone, shattered, heartbroken at the loss of his bosom friend, with his last security blanket torn away. All persons upon whom David might lean were ripped from his life. Jonathan returned home. David went away.

What *does* one do when every vestige of human security is gone?

God can create a squash in weeks. For an oak, He may take a century. He will not put a squash on the throne. Maybe an oak! In this stripping, God was seasoning a king for a throne, but at least for a time David lost sight of God's plan. Overwhelmed by grief, fear and despair, David fled again, this time alone, and in panic.

Caving In

For several senseless months, David ran amuck. He had lost his position and the people upon whom he had leaned because God took them away. Then David made some bad choices himself and gave away the rest of what is precious to a person.

At a place called Nob, David gave away his *integrity* (1 Samuel 21:1-9). He tried to shape God to fit his own needs. For the first time David failed to inquire of the Lord. Panic drove him. Nothing steered him. *To the desert. Food. I've got to have food. And a weapon; I didn't even bring a weapon. Where? Oh, to the priests at Nob. They'll have supplies. What will I tell them?*

Lies. "I'm on the king's business. My men? Hiding near. Yes, they can eat the sacred food." More lies to cover lies. David was beginning to sound quite a lot like Saul.

"Only Goliath's sword? Yes, I swing that well, remember?"

Who is that by the gate? Looks like Doeg, Saul's chief shepherd, Saul's chief spy. I must hurry. What will happen to the priests when Saul finds out? Never mind, no time to worry about that now.

When Saul arrived at Nob, his jealous rage, plus David's selfish lies, would soak the soil of that village with the blood of priests and women and children. Oh, dreadful loss! Integrity caved in.

If David lost his integrity at Nob, he lost his *dignity* at Gath. When integrity goes, sooner or later dignity follows. David fled blindly to Gath. The Philistine capital. Home of Goliath. Oh, no, David, what are you thinking about? Anywhere but Gath!

What is this? David, do you wonder where you are? The streets are buzzing. They are quoting the war song, "David [has slain] his tens of thousands." Those were Philistines you killed, David. You are crazy to have come here. Insane! *Insane. That's it. I'll throw them off and save my neck by pretending I'm psychotic. Here comes King Achish. I'd better make this good.*

Oh, David. Shepherd close to the heart of God. Majestic warrior. King elect — this can't be you. Clothes dirty and askew, the wild look in your eye. Why is that spit dribbling from your mouth and slithering down your beard? What is the meaning of your animal-like scratching on the gates?

Confusion

Why does confusion make us think we can find solace in the camp of the enemy? We panic and play the fool; we do stupid things.

- We get ourselves into financial difficulty. Then, in a fit of self-pity, we go on a spending binge to make ourselves feel better. Stupid!

- Distance is growing between them. She's hurt by her husband's lack of attention. In fact, another woman seems to be getting it. So she nags at him and screams at him in a panicky attempt to make him love her. Stupid!

- His business is threatened. He can scarcely stay up with the field, let alone keep his finger in all the pies. He is so depressed that he takes to drinking heavily to feel better. He only deepens his depression and further impairs his ability to do business. Stupid.

- She is depressed, so she sleeps late, and the work gets behind. This makes her feel worse. She stays up later because she can't sleep. Pills finally put her down in the wee hours. She wakes up even later, further behind, more depressed. Stupid, vicious cycle. Stop it!

My feigned madness is working. Achish feels there are already too many crazies in Gath. Here's my chance. Run for it. Run!

So David ran. He literally ran to a cave. He caved in. Position, people, integrity, dignity, all gone. It seemed he couldn't go on. Trapped, at the end of the rope, in a cave. Not just any cave, mind you, but the cave of Adullam, a labyrinth of caves, tunnels, and secret places, covering hundreds of rocky desert acres, like some giant sinister molehill. Adullam is a secure place to hide in all right, but it is gloomy, dark and lonely, and is occupied by brigands, bats, serpents and wild beasts. Later Adullam served as hiding places for Christians under the sword. Today guides fear the place. A man could lose himself there and never get out.

Coming Out of the Cave

Are you in a cave? No more places to run? No heart to go on? The inscription at the head of Psalm 142 claims it was written by David when he was in the cave:

No one is concerned for me.
  I have no refuge;
no one cares for my life (verse 4).

David, you seem to be about as low as a man can get. I've been there, too. Millions have. Everyone seems gone. Everything seems lost. No one cares. There seems nowhere to turn. Some take pills or jump from the bridge or pull the trigger. Others crawl farther into the cave and pull the hole in after them — dragging along a bottle or a television set. You have stumbled into those houses that look like caves. One cave I visited houses an old, broken-down, professional athlete with his shabby live-in girlfriend, flea-bitten dog, drawn shades, whiskey bottles and cocaine. Lonely widows, or self-pitying divorced people, or bored retirees rot in other caves. Some make their church their cave.

These all miss the point of the cave. Not David. One thing about David which keeps me coming back to him is that he kept coming back to God. He never permanently gave up on their relationship.

Oh, David, you give me the heart to go on. You hit me with the cattle-prod of new beginnings. You came back to your senses. Listen to the rest of the cave-psalm:

I cry to you, O LORD;
  I say, "You are my refuge,
my portion in the land of the living."
  Listen to my cry . . .
Set me free from my prison
          (Psalm 142:5-7).

David emerged from his cave. Check out his exit route: **First**, *David looked up*. He recovered his security by reopening dialogue with God. In this way he recovered the only real security anyone will ever know.

In former days David had lived in constant dialogue with God. God was his security, his light, his strength, his integrity. God's presence had been as real to David as the wilderness and the wind; their conversation as natural as breathing. In the valley of Elah, God fought beside David to defeat the giant. Even the priests of Nob, arguing for their lives with Saul, testify that David frequently inquired of the Lord (see 1 Samuel 22:15). But at some point that dialogue had stopped. David failed to inquire of God before he lied to the priests of Nob. He wrote no psalm of faith and praise on his insane journey to Gath. Ah, but from the darkness of the cave, David once again "inquired of the LORD" (1 Samuel 23:2). He looked up.

Second, *David came clean.* He recovered his integrity by facing the ugly facts of his failures. *Who is that stumbling into my cave? Abiathar!* He has run all night from Nob carrying a few sacred objects. "What is the crimson on your hand, Abiathar?"

"Blood, David. Saul killed every priest at Nob. Every wife, every child, even the cattle and sheep. I alone escaped."

Listen to David's reply: "Doeg? I saw him at the gate. I should have known. Abiathar, men, listen! What happened at Nob was my doing. Anyone in his right mind would have known Saul would make Nob pay for helping me—but I was so bent on saving my own skin, I didn't care that my lies jeopardized a whole town. The blood is on my hands." David genuinely repented.

Ours is not to brood over what is taken from us. We can't control that. The best grief is over what we gave away in our blind self-preoccupation. On the way to the cave we make choices. Accepting responsibility for our deceptions and callousness is the first and most indispensable step toward healing.

Third, *David stood tall*. He recovered his dignity when he resumed his God-given leadership and again began acting like a king. The cave-psalm ends: "Then the righteous will gather about me" (verse 7).

The Way of Recovery

They did. To the cave of Adullam came hundreds of people hungry for David's leadership. David's family came. Distressed men and indebted men came to David needing protection and money. Discontented men came, too—former officers of Saul. They would follow David. From this odd collection God sent him, David forged an army of more than six hundred men.

When a man has truly faced his mistakes and knows the forgiveness of God, he is secure in God—but only in God. Then something about him often attracts the loyalty, admiration, and love of courageous and distressed and penitent people. There is no need to wallow in our mire all of our days nor to rob the world of our gifts because of past failures. We are too hard on ourselves—and too hard on our very human leaders.

Things began changing for David that day. Securely back in dialogue with God, he had manfully recovered his integrity. His dignity returned also, along with his security. Once more he stood tall.

Notice, however, his circumstances had changed little. True, he came out of the cave of Adullam, but he was still a fugitive in the Judean deserts. Saul still pursued him relentlessly. He was still betrayed by the treachery of people he protected. Those things hadn't changed. It was the important things that were different. David's whole attitude changed because his identity was restored. He was God's man.

From Adullam David moved to En Gedi. If Adullam is the armpit of the world, En Gedi is the smile on her face. Here, high above the western shores of the Dead Sea, tumble streams of clear fresh water, forming a paradise of five majestic cataracts. A steep trail leading up from the Dead Sea rises through this lush green oasis. My wife Carolyn and I climbed this trail. Leaving the hot desert behind, we waded and splashed in some of the pools fed by plumelike waterfalls, surrounded by flowers and ferns, and canopied at places by reeds. No doubt David and his wives frolicked in these very pools. In this stronghold he found refreshing respite from the stench of Adullam and from the desert heat.

Come out. Come out of your cave. You can! Look up. Trust the only one worthy of trust. Come clean. Honestly repent. Stand tall. Get out of your cave and on with God's task for you. After your Adullam, He may lead you to your En Gedi.

When you've lost everything,
and no one seems to care about you
Remember:
You still have someone to go to
who always cares.

But David thought to himself,
"One of these days I will be destroyed
by the hand of Saul.
The best thing I can do
is to escape to the land of the Philistines.
Then Saul will give up searching for me
anywhere in Israel, and I will slip
out of his hand."
So David and the six hundred men with him
left and went over to Achish
son of Maoch king of Gath.
—1 Samuel 27:1,2

FOUR

*Three steps that will help you, as they did David,
to come back from being out of touch with God,
in a hostile land . . .*

Running From Our Roots

1 Samuel 27–30

ou may be reading these words while
on the road. You are following your job
in a strange town. No one knows you.
You are tempted to get lost in the
bright lights or the dark streets. You
have no real social context, no friends
to answer to, no one who cares what
you do, much less what you think. If
this is the case, you may be in deadly spiritual peril!

Possibly you have been bombarded by a sec-
ular environment all week. Vicious competitiveness.
Driving ego. Crass materialism. All week long! The
environment is hostile to faith, both because there is

little time or opportunity to feed your faith and because people laugh at you for believing. You also may be spiritually lonely, having no fellow believer to share with for days on end. Small wonder you become distracted, pragmatic, even confused.

This happened to David, too. After he spared Saul's life a second time, Saul went home, the book says, but David "went on his way" (1 Samuel 26:25b). Something vague and rootless hangs over those words, *went on his way*. To where?

For years the tenacious pursuit of his enemy kept him moving. The constant threat of death and the demands for survival in a hostile land pressed him toward a pit of exhaustion. David was ground down to a vulnerable state. On the run in this strange land, he was losing contact with the solid things which would remind him of who he was. David ran from his roots till he was out of touch. Incredibly, at this point, David decided to go join the enemy. Why?

Out of Touch

Once outside familiar structure, David became a law to himself. Hebrew village routine no longer shaped him. No appointments to keep, no superiors to please, no institutions to support, no expectations to meet. David, cut off from his roots, was also distanced from the people of Judah. He was hurt and disillusioned and had been betrayed by his relatives.

Having been hurt by people you love, are you away from family, with no church home and no one to be accountable to? Does it seem easy to lose your way?

Besides being outside structure and cut off from his roots, David was virtually out of touch with

God. For three chapters of the Bible (covering sixteen months) no prayers are recorded by David. There is no "inquiring of the LORD," as was his custom. No songs are even sung by David, much less written, during these rootless months. He doesn't mention God. His heart and his pen both seem dry. David wandered in the land of the Philistines feeling what the Israelites expressed later: "How can we sing the songs of the LORD while in a foreign land?" (Psalm 137:4).

Have you been there, too? I have. An early symptom of my distancing from God was that I lost my song. My lips quit singing because the music inside me had died.

Sometimes, the fact that we are not praising God does not occur to us. He is out of sight, out of mind. The next step is inevitable. We become sitting ducks for bad choices.

Bad Choices

When David was out of touch, he made bad choices. **First**, he *chose wrong attitudes*. We don't ordinarily speak of choosing our attitudes. We "have" attitudes, "get" attitudes, or "drift into" attitudes – but "choose" them? We don't like the ring of that. Yet an attitude is a choice. Attitudes don't just happen to us.

David chose to become self-centered and self-protective. He "thought to himself, *the best thing I can do is to escape*" (1 Samuel 27:1a). No reflecting on God's will here nor dependence on divine resources. His purpose is no longer God's plan for him, or the good of the kingdom, but rather saving his own hide – so that he might "slip out of the hand of Saul" (verse 1b). Selfishness and self-thinking lead inevitably to depression and self-pity. *One of these days,* lamented David, *I will be destroyed.* Negativism really is a lack of trust in God.

Next, David *chose to travel.* Rather than go deeper into the heart of his home country, he headed toward the heart of Philistia, to Gath. How can one get to the right place by going in the wrong direction? He went to Achish and eventually settled in Ziklag. How quickly we become attached. Before long the king of Gath is saying that David "will be my servant forever" (1 Samuel 27:12).

Then, choosing a wrong attitude and going in the wrong direction led David to *choose the wrong methods.* His men made daily bloody raids on remote and scattered camps and villages to the south of Philistia. Though he actually raided friends and allies of the Philistines, he completely convinced Achish, King of Gath, he was killing the friends and allies of Israel. To cover his backside David totally annihilated every man, woman and child in the villages he raided, lest any accurate report should come to the ears of Achish. Thus, to his lies he added wanton and brutal murder. What a far cry from the clear-eyed, tender-featured shepherd poet of Bethlehem. Even if, as some scholars suggest, David's time in Ziklag was really a tactical move toward his throne, he chose means so vile no exalted end could possibly justify them.

Nixonism

Someone has referred this morality of "ends justify means" as Nixonism. During the dark days of Watergate, Richard Nixon stoutly and repeatedly asserted, "I never did anything wrong." Was he lying? Was he out of touch with reality? No, on both counts.

He was simply asserting that since his cause was just, the means was thereby sanctified. If it was good for America, it was good, even though one had to do criminal things to get it done.

Nixonism hits religious institutions, too. If it is "God's institution," whatever is good for the institution is "good for God." Only a short step leads in some cases to the kind of religious politics where group think overrides concern for broken individuals, while the crimes and conundrums of highly visible leaders are whitewashed to "protect their ministries" or to keep from "bringing reproach upon Christ." Nixonism easily and insidiously creeps into large national parachurch organizations, media ministries, and Christian colleges and seminaries.

Many of us have been Nixonian in our personal integrity at times. In little things. "No," we say to the person on the telephone, "you didn't wake me." Why do we say this? To make him feel more comfortable? To make ourselves seem more approachable? To cover our morning laziness?

Maybe we lie nonmaliciously to cover our sins, in order to "protect our witness" so that "our ministry will not be damaged." Then there are the times we fake it and feign an artificial "joy" to present a persuasive public relations face for "evangelistic purposes." David is not alone in taking the road to Gath in order to get to Jerusalem. Most of us travel this route more often than we realize.

Then David really messed up. When he took the fork in the road which led to Philistia, he entered a sixteen-month period of incredible internal turmoil and external chaos.

Deadly Consequences

In the first place, David did not go to Philistia alone. His two wives and his family went along. He also took his army of six hundred men. This ill-advised decision placed many people in jeopardy. While he and his men were off at war, the Amalekites attacked the camp at Ziklag, carrying off the wives and families of David and his men. David's folly put other lives at risk. No doubt in the hands of a violent and amoral people like the Amalekites, the women were ravished and abused. Fatal decisions are never completely our own business.

Even more significantly, David placed a host of people in spiritual jeopardy. The sensual and idolatrous Philistine environment was overwhelmingly appealing. In addition, by choosing his course of lies, violence and self-trust, David himself was modeling all the wrong things for his followers.

Carnality is contagious and has deadly fallout even on the innocent. We prize our independence. Like Frank Sinatra, we boast, "I did it my way." We assert, "I'm a grown boy, and I'll take my own lumps." But reality doesn't work that way. We are part of the fabric of our peer groups, and our direction affects the profile of the entire lot. Besides, there are always those who are younger in years or newer in the faith who will imitate our lifestyles. Of course, those who are parents definitely affect their own children.

While we may feel alone, we never sin alone. The chain reaction of consequences endangers countless people around us, as surely as circles ripple outward from a rock thrown in a pond until they encompass a surface area a thousand times larger than the actual water struck by the rock. Ask the families and peers of Jeb McGruder, Richard Clindeinst, Robert Haldeman, Josh Erlichman, Lawrence Obrian, E. Howard Hunt, G. Gordon Liddy, Charles Colson . . . and Richard M. Nixon.

David's wrong decision also neutralized his own witness. Even King Achish of Gath saw that David had become "odious" to his own people in Judah (1 Samuel 27:12). So stripped of credibility was David that even his own six hundred loyal fighting men, on the brink of mutiny, talked of stoning him to death (1 Samuel 30:6).

Our lives are not our own business. The very essence of life is a treasure from God, intended for the use of influencing the world toward God. Thus with squandered days and misdirected objectives, not only have we failed, but we have actually cast our forces on the side of the enemy. We have become part of the problem rather than part of the solution.

Confusing Duplicity

Worst of all, David seems at times to have so blurred the lines that he became confused about his own self-identity. He attempted to be Philistine on the outside and Israelite on the inside. Tell me, did David make a good decision? The bottom line was: David finally found himself marching in the army of the Philistines on its way to attack Israel (1 Samuel 29:1).

What had David's prolonged distance from the people of God done to him? Surely his mind spun wildly that day as his feet tromped up and down toward the tail of the Philistine ranks. Was he watching for the opportunity to cut and run? Had he read the mood of the Philistine officers that sooner or later they would demand he be sent back home? Or was he ready, finally, to fight against Saul? Or maybe he was plotting to turn on the Philistines in the thick of battle. Probably he was so confused and trapped that he thought of all of the above. He had lived in Philistia with duplicity and without spiritual context and accountability for so long that he wasn't sure who he was any more.

Nixonism distorts us. It is possible to attempt God's business by worldly strategies until we drift over the line and lose sight of who we are. Some have gone over to the world's turf for evangelistic purposes. So far, so good. Then they go on to sit in the bar in order to witness — and some such would-be "relevant evangelists" wind up drunk.

A friend decided to leave the ministry "in order to make my witness more relevant," he said. Besides, he had the opportunity to make a lot of money so he would be able to give a lot to Christian projects and eventually to support his own ministry — he said. This would give him more freedom to be effective, more integrity, and thus, more credibility — he said. So far, so good. But the freedom got to him. And the money and the power. Rather than his effectiveness being broadened and deepened, now my friend is fairly wealthy, divorced — and alcoholic. As with David, the whole thing has become disastrous, and it will stay that way unless somehow God calls him back to his own Ziklag and to sanity.

A favorite Civil War legend has it this way. As Sherman made his relentless march to the sea, somewhere in Georgia he hit a snag. Suddenly, out from behind a rural smokehouse, popped a weary little old lady. Loose strands of her silvery hair floated around her face. Her soiled apron hung at odd angles. But as she planted her feet resolutely, her eyes flashed Dixie fire, and her bony hands brandished a ragged broom. Sherman, astride his magnificent steed, hesitated, then attempted to spur his horse on past her. She attacked, flailing away with all her might. When she stopped for a breather, the amused Sherman said, "Ma'am, don't you see that I am a general on horseback with a whole army behind me and that you are a woman, alone, on foot, with only a broom in your hands? You have no chance even to impede my progress."

"Shucks, I know that, son," snapped the little old lady. "I just wanted to make sure everyone understands which side I'm on."

The trouble with a person wanting to be Christian yet looking carnal is that no one ever quite knows where he is. Eventually, even he himself doesn't know—am I a Philistine or an Israelite?

Bouncing Back

For three biblical chapters and sixteen months David was in a far country, looking and acting like a Philistine. The whole fiasco finally came down on his head, and that day God called him back to sanity.

When David and his men topped the last hill above Ziklag, eager to see their wives and families, rather than being greeted by the laughter of their children, they saw nothing but charred ruins and curls of smoke. Not a person was in sight.

O, my Abigail, and the kids. Are they dead? Maybe alive is worse! Abused by smelly Amalekite lust?

After the initial frantic shouting of names and digging through ashes, David and his stunned men huddled in a circle, their weeping swelling into a wail that lasted till evening. Then the grief in the tortured eyes of the soldiers changed to knowing looks focused on David. Angry hands reached for missiles to fling at him. Mutiny! The time had come for David to operate in the will of God rather than wing it in the flesh where the end justifies the means until the means lose sight of the end. Again he found the heart to go on. "David found strength in the LORD his God" (1 Samuel 30:6).

He began to bounce back.

First, David *reestablished contact with God.* During his spiritual sabbatical, God had been sent to the sidelines and David's strength had drained away. Now his strength revived. Once more, he began calling on God (1 Samuel 30:7,8). This was long overdue. The Lord had not led David to Philistia.

When we find ourselves in a far country, out of touch and out of control, the first step toward recovery is always a reopening of the lines of communication between ourselves and God. Back to basics, to fundamentals.

No matter the circumstances or how dark and threatening the mists and mountains of the far country, the first priority is "inquire of God." Get back in touch, else things will spin ever more hopelessly out of control. David, once settled into the first priority, was able then to clearheadedly make the rest of the needed corrections. Isn't God good? He will take back the children who have lived so long where they shouldn't have been.

Second, David *reestablished his relationhips with the people of God* (1 Samuel 30:26-30). David sent gifts to the elders of Judah. This put him back inside structure, restoring order to his life.

Finding ourselves again after we have lost our way demands getting involved once more with an organized group of believers. A church. An accountability group. Something.

Sometimes I travel alone. In strange cities, when away from my context, if I feel vulnerable to spiritual or moral vertigo, I will call friends to establish contact and ask for assurance and accountability. I feel spiritually safe when I have kept myself accountable to my family and my church—to someone.

Third, once David had reopened his conversation with God and reestablished his relationship with the people of God, he *resumed his role as a leader appointed by God* (1 Samuel 30:9,21-25). He got back to business. He mobilized his six hundred men and set out in pursuit of the Amalekites. He corrected the troublemakers in his ranks who did not want to divide the spoils of battle. Initially, David may well have been planning, via the circuitous Philistine route, to make his way toward the throne. Then he lost his bearings and began to look more like Saul than like David. Now he had recovered his kingly behavior and identity and was ready for Hebron and the throne.

A clear sense of identity brings us a clear sense of responsibility. The story is told that long ago, a popular European monarch, fearing his power would go to his head, asked his most trusted advisors to regularly whisper in his ear, "Remember. You are just a mortal."

Most of us need exactly the opposite. So that we do not live beneath our identity and thus beneath our destiny, we need often to be reminded, "Remember. You are not just mortal!" God is always reminding us of our immortality through Jesus. He does not chide us for our perversities, but challenges us with our possibilities. The Master, His finger under our chin, lifts our eyes to His, whispering, "Remember who you are."

Sometimes clear principles march out of the centuries straight into the thick of daily living. Some are clear here:

Rootlessness leaves one vulnerable to self-deception.

A consistently violated conscience leads to a confused identity.

God's forgiveness and strength are always available when one chooses to come back home.

There is a homeland where you belong, and you must decide if you're in it. If you are wandering in a strange land, why not come on home?

When you feel you have lost your identity,
Remember:
God is always waiting to welcome you home.

And David became famous . . .
He put garrisons throughout Edom . . .
The LORD gave David victory
everywhere he went.

David reigned over all Israel . . .
Joab son of Zeruiah was over the army;
Jehoshaphat son of Ahilud was recorder;
Zadok son of Ahitub and
Ahimelech son of Abiathar were priests;
Seraiah was secretary;
Benaiah son of Jehoiada
was over the Kerethites and Pelethites;
and David's sons were royal advisers.
—2 Samuel 8:13-18

*Five revealing questions David might ask you
about your career . . .*

"When I Get My Ducks in a Row"

2 Samuel 2–10

udie's double-breasted power suits always fit him well, touched off by just the right color tie. He walks briskly, rarely sits still, and looks too serious for a man of 28. He usually sits near the back of the church and has little time for anything not connected with his career.

Tuesday morning over breakfast, Audie said it well for hundreds of others, "I am now in the high-demand time of life. When I have it made and reach my goals, life will be simpler, more manageable. Then I'll be free to be what God wants me to be and to do what He wants done. But first I gotta get my ducks in a row."

🜲 The Dream of a Simple Life

This dream deludes all age groups. High school people voice it—college students, too. Young mothers cling to this illusion. Budding professionals and midlife businessmen often live on this assumption. Occasionally I have heard it even from the lips of retired people.

Does it work that way?

The opening scene of 2 Samuel finds a young Amalekite, with face bloody and clothes tattered, running into Ziklag. Falling before David, he breathlessly reported, "Saul is dead. Jonathan is dead. On Mount Gilboa! The archers got Jonathan. And I found Saul wounded, leaning on his weapon. So I put him out of his misery. Here is his crown."

From that day on, the fortunes of David began another long and meteoric rise. The Lord told David to go up from Ziklag to Hebron of Judah, and "there they anointed David king over the house of Judah" (2 Samuel 2:4). Judah was the smaller tribe in the south. From the north loomed the much larger and more powerful kingdom of Israel, where Saul had reigned. David did not merely snap his fingers and step to the throne of Israel. The long, bitter, in-house battle ground on between Saul's family and David. Blood and intrigue swirled around David. It's not easy to become a king, and David's ascent was not smooth.

Ish-bosheth, son of Saul, sat briefly on Israel's throne, but only by the wits of his general, Abner.

Apparently Abner was a man of great character and charisma. He had commanded Saul's forces before he served Ish-bosheth. Bad blood ran between David's general Joab and Abner.

> Then Abner said to Joab, "Let's have some of
> the young men get up and fight hand to hand
> in front of us" . . . Then each man grabbed his
> opponent by the head and thrust his dagger
> into his opponent's side, and they fell down
> together (2 Samuel 2:14-16).

Abner, disgusted with Ish-bosheth, visited with David one day and offered a pact to bring the northern tribes over to David's side. With the bargain struck, David sent Abner toward home in peace, or so David thought.

Blood and Tears

Enter bloody Joab, full of intrigue. In Abner, Joab saw a major threat to his own high position with David. So after Abner left David's quarters "in peace," Joab staged a friendly greeting outside, then treacherously pulled a dagger at close range, stabbed Abner in the belly, and left him to die in the dirt by the road.

Had Abner lived, David would have gained the northern tribes in a bloodless coup, but by assassinating Abner, Joab further inflamed the already ugly political situation. David led his people to Abner's funeral, walking behind the casket and weeping aloud, saying, "A prince and a great man has fallen in Israel this day" (2 Samuel 3:38).

The path to David's glory was bathed with blood and tears. Mark it well. Upward mobility in every age exacts its toll.

Next, two rascals, Recab and Baanah, in attempting to score points with David, slipped into the house of Ish-bosheth one day and murdered him in his bed. Then they eagerly reported to David, "We have rid you of your last enemy. The throne of Israel is yours." Whether David had wanted this blood or not, these two murderers cleared the way for him to consolidate the two thrones of Judah and Israel into one: "When all the elders of Israel had come to King David at Hebron . . . they anointed David king over Israel" (2 Samuel 5:3).

 ### Reaching the Top

David finally reached the pinnacle.

Far to the north stretched all the lands of Israel. Judah spread across the deserts to the south. In the very center between the two domains, on the top of a high mountain, stood the city of Jebus. This city, occupied by strangers, was valuable to David because it was politically neutral, aligned with neither north nor south. The city of Jebusites was thought to be impregnable—defensible on all sides, but a water shaft tunneled down and out from under the walls. At great risk Joab and his men swam the water tunnel, scaled its shaft and overthrew the Jebusites (see 2 Samuel 5:6-9 and 1 Chronicles 11:4-7).

The city called Jebus, then Salem, now became Jebus-Salem—or Jerusalem—the city of David. This neutral center unified the once warring factions of all Israel and Judah, and it became uniquely David's own city.

So David rose to his days of human glory. Power. Wealth. Freedom. Popularity. All had become his—but life at the top was still no bowl of cherries for David. The expansion of his wealth, popularity and power only brought more problems. Pressure continued to mount. David solidified his alliances with many neighboring countries by taking foreign wives. More relationships to manage, and more sons to go wrong—and go wrong they did.

Tribute flowed into David's coffers from powerful allies and frightened vassals, making David richer by the month. He captured millions of dollars worth of bronze, silver and gold, along with swords, jewelry and shields, bringing it all to storehouses in Jerusalem and dedicating it to the Lord. Accounting became a nightmare. David was forced to become an expert in the monetary systems of the world.

National Expansion

Stiffened opposition required David to escalate his nation's military sophistication. Then he went on expansion offensives of his own. His thousands of foot-soldiers and chariots rumbled away from Jerusalem in every direction, conquering one kingdom after another, and his empire sprawled all the way to the Euphrates River. The Lord gave David victory everywhere he went, and eventually he occupied more than nine hundred square miles of territory. Garrisons built throughout the empire controlled all the major trade routes of the ancient world. As much as 90 percent of the world's wealth came under David's scepter.

How complicated life had become for this once simple shepherd boy. Finances. Construction. Administration. Transportation. Military maneuvers. Political subtleties. Many wives. Many children. More subjects.

More men. More wars. More construction projects. More alliances to maintain. What happened to "the simple life at the top"? In the days of his youth, had David ever collapsed, exhausted at the end of a hard day of shearing sheep, and mused, "If only I could just get my ducks in a row, life would be so much simpler"?

The View From the Top

Even though David finally "got out of college," "built a business," "got his career on the road," and "reached the top of the heap," life did not get any simpler.

Problems multiplied on every front. External forces roared over him like a Niagara. Rivalry, rape, revenge, and revolt ripped at David's family, breaking his heart and undermining his control. In the midst of all this, when he was answerable to no one, David fell prey to the horrendous temptations that attend absolute power.

What do these realities mean for us now?

Take this from a "big mouth": After fifty years of living, I have earned the right to say this. Life does not get simpler.

- You move up the socio-economic ladder.
- Upward mobility deals you more power.
- You realize more of your goals.
- You get to the top.
- You become successful.
- You emerge into greater visibility.
- Your life becomes increasingly complex.

Your vocation, your business, your profession itself becomes more demanding. The pace quickens. Responsibilities expand. Complexity thickens. Volume swells. The stakes become higher. More people—and things—demand your time: administration, employees, public relations, staying current. Community responsibilities proliferate. You are invited onto a multiplicity of boards and committees. Your phone doesn't stop ringing. You are obliged to contribute to a growing list of good causes and required to be sociable with a broadening circle of acquaintances. Just buying wedding and graduation gifts and writing thank-you notes will run you up the wall. You will be expected to show up at more events—when you get your ducks in a row.

As you get older, your family grows larger, older and more expensive, and relationships are more difficult to manage. They lean on you more for help in decisions like college, career and marriage. Your money is stretched ever more tightly as you have one eye on retirement, the other on tuition, tuxedos and trouble, and helping kids start businesses, and buying cars, and providing insurance, and dressing in style.

Temptation will not diminish either. It will only grow. Ask David. As a kid, I asked an older friend, "When you get to be 40 years old, does sexual temptation diminish?"

He replied, "I didn't know anything about sexual temptation until I hit 40."

When you are "in charge" of your world—with money, power, access, visibility, freedom of movement, and lack of accountability—sexual temptations take on dramatic new dimensions. Money, sex and power can easily twist the finest soul.

Have I made it sound tough enough yet?

🪷 Illusions

The assumptions of my friend Audie in the opening lines of this chapter are not really assumptions. They are illusions.

"When I have made it, I'll have time for . . . " How was that again?

"I want to make a lot of money for God. I must make money now so I can give money later." What was that again?

A farmer was explaining to a minister, "Well, if I'd get enough, I'd give half to the Lord."

"If you had two thousand acres of oil wells," asked the preacher, "would you give revenues from one thousand acres to the Lord?"

"Why, sure," the farmer gloated. "Anyone could live off a thousand acres of oil."

"If you had two hogs, would you give one to the Lord?" queried the minister.

At that, the farmer complained, "That's not fair. You know I have two pigs!"

We don't suddenly, someday, have an abundance of time and money to give. We begin with the little pieces. We are in training now, learning bit by bit to manage money, power, time, relationships and temptation. Then maybe someday we will find ourselves competent to manage life on a grander scale.

Remember my friend who said he wanted to leave the ministry to expand his witness? As years passed, the money and the power became increasingly important to him. Power accessed a world of distractions. Now his life is a shambles. There is no ministry. The pressures ate him alive.

These things got David, too — except when he kept in touch with God and accountable to good people. David was at his best when:

- he was singing;
- he was praying;
- he inquired of the Lord;
- he surrounded himself with wise counselors and men of God.

The rest of the time David was in trouble. He lived approximately seventy years. From 17 till 30, he was on the run. From 30 till 50, his life was a triumph. From 50 till 70, his life was a tragedy. Life is not going to get easier for us as we get older, either.

What's Really Important

Must one reach the top in order to be a useful and successful human being? There is nothing wrong with the top for some people — but search your heart to its depths. What price are you willing to pay for the illusions of success? What can you afford to put on hold in the meantime?

Ask yourself, "Do I actually have the gifts, brains and energy to do this for God, and still be able to sing, pray, call upon God, and listen to wise counselors? Or am I reaching beyond my capabilities?"

Parents, are you putting pressure on your children to achieve what was important to you, while your children may have better dreams? Or is your example like an attorney I know who left a lucrative practice to work as an assistant D.A., at much less money, so he could help effectively prosecute child abusers and wife beaters?

We live near a university. Frequently, these days, I see students, who earlier had earned degrees in the high-paying professions and become "successful," returning for graduate work. Empty of everything but success, they are now coming and enrolling in the social work courses, or marriage and family, or pre-med, or ministry. They are more interested in the humanities and the service professions because they have found better dreams.

Could a healthy family be a worthwhile goal in itself?

A young man with three children recently confided to me that he had changed the whole direction of his vocation because, he said, "When they write the words on my tombstone, I want them to remember my children, not my career. So I have decided my children will be my career."

Five Questions

Should I quit deluding myself with dreams of future simplicity and spirituality, and instead, just live every day like I ought to live now?

Slow down. In fact, read each of the following questions slowly. Ponder them separately. They are questions a beleaguered David might want you to consider. Why not actually turn to the inside of the back cover of this book and jot down your answers there?

- Am I learning to be responsible with time, money and freedom now?

- Am I calling on God — now? Am I singing and praying — now?

- Do I make myself accountable — now? Am I surrounded with godly friends and counselors now?

- Am I building strong relationships with my mate and my children now?

- Is my house a place of hospitality and service now? If not, it will not likely warm up later.

Only the most superficial of fools could miss the point of what was going on during the power years of David's life. Only the most gullible and self-deluded can dream that life will become simpler with time and as we move up the ladder.

Now is the time to hunger for God with all of our hearts. Today is the day to be the kind of people we dream of becoming when we get our "ducks in a row"!

When career pressures are
getting you down,
Remember:
God can help you find the real values
in your heart and show you how to
change your life to reflect them.

Ascribe to the LORD, O mighty ones,
ascribe to the LORD glory and strength.
Ascribe to the LORD the glory due his name;
worship the LORD
in the splendor of his holiness.
—Psalm 29:1,2

David helps us see and understand a little more
of God's awesome holiness . . .

God of Death and God of Dancing

2 Samuel 6
1 Chronicles 15

he name Dennis Wise epitomizes Elvis
Presley fan clubs. Wise's love for Elvis
has driven him to bizarre lengths. He
even had his face lifted and his hair-
line contoured by a plastic surgeon to
make himself look like Presley. Wise
explained his passion to reporters:

Presley has been an idol ever since I was five
years old. I have every record he ever made and
pictures in the thousands. I even have a couple of
books in Japanese and Chinese and some leaves
from his front yard.

91

No sir. I never saw Elvis personally. I saw
him on the stage four times. I stood up on the
wall at Graceland once for twelve hours trying to
get a glimpse of him. But he had so many people
around I could never get close.

The adoration of Dennis Wise for Elvis Presley approaches worship. Words like these belong to the
worship of God. Reshaping the face sounds like Paul
urging Christians to be changed into the image of
Christ. Gathering artifacts is something that we God-
worshipers have done for centuries.

Yet poor Dennis Wise never really knew Elvis
or even got close enough to really see him. He was kept
away by walls and by other people. How unlike God
Presley's bulwarks were! We are not separated from
God by a twelve-foot wall nor need we buy any fifteen-
dollar ticket to watch Him perform. Yet one would wish
many people could discover a holy reverence for God
even remotely akin to the feeling Dennis Wise has for
Elvis Presley.

Human beings are worshipers. We will give
our devotion to something. Unfortunately, in our day
we seem to want a God who is answerable to us. Sometimes we treat Him as if He were a giant bubble-gum
machine: Insert coin and collect goodies. We will not
allow God to do things we don't understand. He must
explain Himself to our satisfaction or we are not sure
we want to believe in Him. After all, we do not want a
God who might ask of us the difficult, unreasonable or
painful.

In short, we want God to be a good luck charm
that we carry into the tough times of life to give us what
we want without any regard to what He wants!

The Ark of God and Death

Perhaps poor Uzzah might grab our attention. Seeing the ark of God about to fall off a cart, Uzzah reached out his hand to steady it and God struck him dead. A Sunday school child complained, "That is the meanest God I could imagine. Why, I remember once when Mother's best china plate was falling off the table. When I reached out to grab it, she didn't spank me; she doubled my allowance! But God killed Uzzah for trying to protect God's china plate."

At first glance, we understand the child's feelings — until we examine this incident in more depth.

What was the "ark of God," anyway? The word *ark* means a "box" or a "chest," but the ark of God was no ordinary box. It was not impressively large, being only three feet nine inches long and two feet three inches wide and two feet three inches high. Yet for the ancient Hebrews, this chest was the most sacred of artifacts.

The ark contained three objects: a gold jar of the miraculous manna which had fallen from heaven when God fed Israel in the wilderness; Aaron's walking stick, or "rod," which had miraculously budded long after it was a dead piece of wood; and (the big items) the tablets of stone on which the Ten Commandments were written.

On the gold-covered lid of the ark was the "mercy seat," where gold cherubim looked in and down, from either end, toward the Law. This space was the focal point where Yahweh, the almighty God of the universe, came to meet His people (2 Samuel 6:2,3).

So sacred was the ark that no one was to touch it, nor even to look into it, upon pain of death.

Incredibly, this most sacred object had been left gathering dust at Shiloh for a number of years. During that time, the people had lost the sense of fear and wonder they once held regarding the ark. Dust also collected on their souls. Then came war with the feared Philistines. Desperate for a good luck charm to protect them, the Israelites dusted off the ark of God and dragged it into battle.

This did not mean they intended to repent and become God's faithful people. Rather, their philosophy was, "We will live wickedly and selfishly, but when we get into a fight, we can invoke God and He will win the battle for us. We can take Him along in His little gold box."

When they found themselves losing, with at least four thousand men dead, the Israelites called time out, scratching their heads and wondering what had gone wrong. "We thought arks were supposed to win wars." When they headed back into the battle the second time, thirty thousand more people died in their defeat. Most terrifying of all, the little box with the big God was carried away into the land of the Philistines.

The terror never let up. The ark brought such grief to the Philistines that they shunned it like a live grenade. Loading it on an oxcart, the Philistines sent it on its way home. As the ark arrived at Beth Shemesh, the Israelites hastily erected an altar of stone, smashed the cart into firewood, cut the oxen into pieces, and offered them as a sacrifice of gratitude. The ark of God was back home.

Their joy was born of selfishness, though, not of awe for the holy one. In their very act of exuberance they broke the law and desecrated the ark merely by looking over into it, and seventy men were struck dead. Frightened and confused, they put the awful thing in storage at the house of Abinadab, where it stayed for more than twenty years.

The Ark and David

Then David took the city of Jerusalem and ascended to the throne. The man after God's own heart couldn't wait to bring the ark of God to the center of his city.

God's presence was in the ark. David wanted "The Presence" secure at the heart of the capital. Israel and Judah had been sharply divided, but now, together, they had a new capital, which was in neither Israel nor Judah. Relocated in Jerusalem, the ark would belong to all the people of God. It would help solidify the kingdom politically as well as religiously.

Yet David recklessly did exactly what the Philistines had done with the ark of God; he actually hauled it on a cart.

As they all set out for Jerusalem, Ahio and Uzzah, sons of Abinadab, walked in the lead with thousands of Israelites in festive procession bringing up the rear. Shouting. Singing. Blasting trumpets, ringing tambourines and beating drums. The ark of God was ascending Mount Moriah.

Then the unthinkable happened — and the party abruptly ended. An ox stumbled, the ark tottered, and Uzzah instinctively put out his hand to steady it.

Wham!

> The LORD's anger burned against Uzzah
> because of his irreverent act; therefore God
> struck him down and he died there beside the
> ark of God (2 Samuel 6:7).

David was stunned. In anger and terror he parked the ark that day at the house of Obed-Edom.

All this raises a couple of scary questions: What is this really about? Why did God strike Uzzah?

The Ark and Irreverence

One reason we have difficulty comprehending why God struck Uzzah is that we ourselves have such an "Uzzah view" of God. Like our ancient Palestinian brothers, we often tend to reduce Jehovah to a good-luck charm in a box.

R. C. Sproul tells the story of a Maryland truck driver arrested for drunk driving. The man was hauled into the magistrate's court, where the judge levied a $100 fine for DWI. The drunk paid his fine but wouldn't leave, and he was so abusive the magistrate added thirty days in jail. Still the drunk's abusive profanity filled the air. Finally the judge rummaged in his law books and came up with a long-forgotten statute that made it a crime to blaspheme in public. He invoked the archaic law, levying another $100 fine and another thirty days in jail.

The press went nuts over this "gross miscarriage of justice." Why should this poor guy have to pay $200 and rot in jail for sixty days simply because he cussed in court? For them, driving a truck while intoxicated was a much larger offense than blaspheming the name of almighty God.[1]

The truck driver should could be grateful that he hadn't come up in the court of Aaron because, by Old Testament law, blasphemy of God carried the death penalty (Numbers 4). In fact, eighteen offenses bearing a death penalty appear in the old law. (One of them is sassing one's parents. I remind my kids of that one.) Not a lawyer in Israel could have gotten that poor truck driver off with only a $200 fine and sixty days in the slammer.

The problem with Uzzah was not that, with good intention, he made a little mistake. Oh, no, Uzzah knew exactly what he was doing. The man was a Levite, a Kohathite, specifically charged (Numbers 4) with caring for the sacred things of the ark. He had to have known about the death penalty.

The caretakers of the ark knew that, in accordance with Exodus 37, on the sides of the sacred box were rings made of gold, through which gold-covered poles were to slide, and only the high priests touched those poles as they carried the ark on their shoulders. Even then they were careful, upon pain of death, not to look at the awesome sacred thing, much less grab it like a packing crate and plunk it down on a cart.

The point was not that the box itself was special, but that it symbolized reverence for the holy God, Yahweh, the almighty of the universe.

Uzzah did not hallow the name of God. This incident is a statement of the awfulness of irreverence – of treating God and sacred things lightly.

Have you touched the ark lately? Trivializing sin is like touching the ark. We don't look at sin through God's eyes. Sin killed His holy Son. For us sin is a foible, a weakness. "I'm only human, you know." We had best admit sin is an affront to the holy God of heaven.

The Bible says, "The soul that sins will die." Any one of us is alive this moment only because of the mercy and grace of a kind and patient God, not because we deserve to live or that the death penalty is inhumane.

Dealing lightly with sacred things is akin to touching the ark. I am astounded, for example, that during communion people sometimes sit and gab, show each other photographs, whisper, and distract those God-hungry souls around them. Some stumble in late, and have to crawl over people. What would happen if God decided to deal with us as He did with Uzzah?

Hans Kung says, "I am not surprised that Uzzah died, but that the rest of us are still alive."[1] We are all sinners. We deserve to die.

We often sing songs containing God's name, addressing God as lackadaisically as if we were caught before the news cameras during "sing time" at Kiwanis Club and were embarrassed not to mouth a few words. When we sing sacred songs halfheartedly, do we deserve Uzzah's lightning bolt?

Possibly we have something to learn from the ancient Hassidic legend of Rabbi Malaki. The eager and devout rabbi prayed fervently and persistently, "Oh, Adonai. Please reveal to me Your true name so that I may know it even as the angels know it." Morning after morning, Malaki raised this petition.

Finally, Adonai honored the old rabbi's request, whereupon Malaki fled and hid under his bed, yelping like a frightened animal and begging Adonai to help him forget *The True Name.*

When we are insensitive to people, we have our hands dangerously close to the ark, folks. At our house we sometimes play a little game. When we have guests, we take special notice that some people take the food being passed around, put some on their own plates and then set the serving dish down, rather than passing it on. Just a minor, superficial thing, you say? Maybe, yet it's a clue to how a person lives his or her whole life. When I am insensitive to God, I am into myself. When I am into myself, I really don't care that much about other people.

How about when we treat the grace of life cheaply, squandering our God-given gifts in a game of trivial pursuit? Is something holy being dishonored? Even in the retirement years? Are not life and its gifts sacred enough that we retire to something?

God's Presence

On our last visit to Israel we met with a little band of Christians in a nondescript building near the center of Jerusalem. Approximately fifty people in a little room, we sat in concentric circles around the communion table that was in the center. People in that assembly came from all over the world. Some had been in prison for their faith. A number had been beaten repeatedly because of Jesus. Bombs have been thrown into their building, and once the building was even burned down—but they have clung to their faith.

We stood up and gathered around the communion table, and with deep emotion, recited first the *Shema:*

Hear, O Israel: the LORD our God, the LORD is
one . . . (Deuteronomy 6:4-9).

Then came the words of the Lord's prayer,
before we took the bread and wine. Tears rolled down
upraised cheeks as lips whispered, "O Adonai." I felt we
indeed stood in the presence of the holy, approaching
the ark of God!

God's Way

But we must move on—and as we do, we
discover that dancing followed death. After the Uzzah
party turned sour, David did some homework. He went
back and checked the fine print in the "Manual for
Caretakers of the Ark." We wonder if he recalled what
Samuel had said to Saul, that obedience is even more
important than sacrifice (see 1 Samuel 15:22).

One can't help admiring those who pay close
attention to the fine print. David's homework is described clearly in 1 Chronicles. He got all the people
together, and he said:

> It was because you, the Levites, did not bring
> [the ark] up the first time that the LORD our
> God broke out in anger against us. We did not
> inquire of him about how to do it in the
> prescribed way (1 Chronicles 15:13).

This time they got down the old family Bible
to check what God wants of those who move arks. No
doubt they reread Exodus 37 about the poles and rings.
They probably also reread Numbers 4 about the Kohathites and touching the ark. They were reminded of the
holy presence of God between the cherubim and above
the mercy seat.

They came back to the ark as changed men. Can you imagine how long it took to work up the nerve to attempt another ark-moving party? Can you see the Kohathites cautiously taking up the gold-covered poles, wiping their hands, again, then once again? Watch as they ease each pole very slowly into its rings, trying not to look at the ark. Then the ark is lifted ever so carefully to their shoulders. The priests cautiously take one step, then two, then three.

Will the bolt of lightning strike?

"Are you ready for the fourth, fellas?"

Five. Six.

"Where is that bull?"

The ark is carefully set down. Then an altar is quickly prepared and a bull is offered. Sacrifice. Checking. Testing. Then tremendous relief when God accepts the sacrifice.

 ## The Ark and Dancing

Then, says the Bible:

> David . . . danced before the LORD with all his
> might, while he and the entire house of Israel
> brought up the ark of the LORD with shouts
> and the sound of trumpets (2 Samuel 6:14).

Oh, I would like to have been there that day. After all David had been through, even after the horror of Uzzah's penalty, out of the genuine joy of his heart, David could dance before God!

One little hitch marred David's celebration. We see in 2 Samuel 6:16 that "as the ark of the LORD was entering the City of David, Michal daughter of Saul watched from a window." Where have we heard of this lady before? Michal was David's first wife, whom David had left behind in escaping from Saul, and she had remarried. This did not deter David. He had taken her back again, and her husband, who appears to have been a wimp, had tagged along behind Michal, weeping, until Abner finally sent the poor fellow back home.

These were not warm and gentle times.

By this time I doubt Michal was a happy bride, although she was in the palace of the king. When she saw David leaping and dancing before the Lord, "she despised him in her heart" (verse 16). She belittled him with:

> How the king of Israel has distinguished
> himself today, disrobing in the sight of the
> slave girls of his servants as any vulgar
> fellow would! (verse 20)

David lost control at this point. "I was worshipping the LORD," he defended; then angrily, no doubt, "who chose me rather than [your daddy] . . . I will celebrate before the LORD." David was willing to be humiliated, or do whatever needed to be done, to properly adore God. Body and soul were thrown into uninhibited praise to the God of death and the God of dancing. Michal was barren from that day on.

Some of us want to be David. Most of us have been Uzzah. I am afraid some of us might want to play Michal—cynical of ourselves, cynical of others, too, unable to accept the legitimacy of anyone else's celebration—because we ourselves don't feel joy or adoration. "If you appear to have enough religion to sing and dance about it, you've got to be phony. Why? Because I have never felt like that."

A co-worker once said to me, "Well, I know you want more staff time for prayer and vulnerability and fellowship with people and devotional Bible study, but I don't need that sort of thing." I discovered later that the person resisting the vulnerability of devotional sharing had disastrous things going on in his own life.

Others may say things like:

- "Oh, those people over there think they are so spiritual."
- "That bunch. All they want to do is pray. Sometimes they'll pray for an hour."
- "What is this stuff? They want this quiet reflection garbage. Some even sing loud and clap their hands."

I may not be into clapping and hand-raising myself, but I dare not play Michal to those who are.

So the ark rested in the city of Jerusalem, bringing with it great fear and great joy because it symbolized the presence of Yahweh.

Today we dare not play Uzzah before God's holiness. When we take the bread, His body, and the wine, His blood, we must beware lest we put our hands on the ark.

Let us also pray that there be no Michals lurking in the corners of our hearts. This is the day to dance up Calvary's hill, like David ascending Mount Moriah, forgiven, singing to the Lord of His goodness, full of heart to go on.

> Ascribe to the LORD, O mighty ones,
>   ascribe to the LORD glory and strength.
> Ascribe to the LORD the glory due his name;

worship the LORD in the splendor of
His holiness (Psalm 29:1).

Have you been a little careless in your
reverence for God?
Remember:
You can experience true joy
through obedience to Him.

David said to Solomon:
"My son, I had it in my heart to build a house
for the Name of the LORD my God.
But this word of the LORD came to me:
'You have shed much blood
and have fought many wars.
You are not to build a house for my Name,
because you have shed much blood
on the earth in my sight.

But you will have a son
who will be a man of peace and rest,
and I will give him rest
from all his enemies on every side.
His name will be Solomon,
and I will grant Israel peace and quiet
during his reign.
He is the one who will build
a house for my Name.
He will be my son, and I will be his father.
And I will establish the throne of his kingdom
over Israel forever.' "
—1 Chronicles 22:7-10

SEVEN

*David teaches us by his example
how to react to disappointment . . .*

Shattered Dreams

2 Samuel 7
1 Chronicles 22

ne lazy day last autumn while dove
hunting with my sons, I walked into
one of those quiet but disturbing in-
terludes. Because the boys wanted to
stay longer than I could, I cut loose
from them and headed across some
rugged pastureland. The trail round-
ed a mesquite clump and brought me up on the site of
an abandoned farmstead, sprawled across the hillside.

Rusted barrels slumbered in tall grass beside
broken-down machinery. The remains of a neat picket
fence had swirled into a jumble of gray sticks. Pigeons

fluttered up from vacant doorways. Sad windows stared like the gaping eyes of a lunatic, as if the house had long since gone mad with loneliness.

I stood there a long time pondering shattered dreams. What dream had brought settlers to this hillside? Had they sketched this place on paper before it actually took form, and had they eagerly talked of it late into their nights? What had they felt as they drove the first nails into this house? Were they warmed with pride the first time friends took dinner with them in their new home?

I couldn't help wondering, also, when they left this house, and why they left, and what they felt that day. Did they savor a long, last look, then turn and lower their blurring eyes as they walked away from their dreams?

Dreams.

> We are all of us dreamers of dreams;
>   On visions our childhood is fed,
> And the heart of a child is undaunted, it seems,
>   By the ghosts of dreams that are dead.
>   — From "To Dream Again"
>   by William Herbert Carruth

Obviously, dreams can turn on us. In fact, very few dreams ever become reality.

The week after my autumn afternoon interlude, I interviewed a number of people, asking them to "tell me about your broken dreams."

One young woman said, "I came to this university to be near my fiance. I thought we would marry at the end of our senior year. We had prayed often about it, and both felt it was the Lord's will. Then, two months before the wedding date, he told me it was off." A shattered dream.

Another student said, "I have always wanted to be a professor of note. But I discovered I am a people person and don't have what it takes to stay alone with the books. Likely I'm stuck at my eight-to-five job for the rest of my life." Dreams died.

An elderly man told of his dream of beginning a Christian college. However, the man he had trusted most embezzled a large sum of money, and the dream went down along with the finances of a number of his friends. "Something inside me was crushed," he reflected.

A woman pushing a walker said, "I always wanted to go to Africa, but I'll never be able to."

Desires of the Heart

What does the Bible mean when it says, "Delight yourself in the LORD and He will give you the desires of your heart" (Psalm 37:4)? Is this an empty promise? If not, why are so many of our compelling desires never realized? Dreams not just growing dim, but shattered, dead, gone.

> We may live on by effort and plan
>   When the fine bloom of living is shed
> But God pity the little that's left of a man
>   When the last of his dreams is dead.
>   —William Herbert Carruth

What is your dream? When the psalmist tells us to delight ourselves in the Lord and He will give us the desires of our hearts, he assumes that delight in God will give our hearts the right kind of desires. As we grow closer to Him, godlike desires shape our dreams. Then our dreams grow too big to be dominated by circumstances, because they are dreams of what God does with a person's heart. Strange. The heart within us is larger than all that is outside us.

🔱 David's Dream

David's dream apparently was born during a quiet season in his life, "after the king was settled in his palace and the LORD had given him rest from all his enemies around him" (2 Samuel 7:1).

> These are the times when dreams are born:
> After the crisis; before the next storm. (L. A.)

Boom! Re-enter Nathan, the prophet. The Bible says little about this disturbing man, yet he is not easily forgotten and he keeps showing up at crucial moments, changing things all around. Apparently Nathan was a close friend of David's. David said to him, "Here I am, living in a palace of cedar, while the ark of God remains in a tent" (verse 2).

Nathan said what good friends usually say, "Whatever you have in mind, go ahead and do it, for the LORD is with you" (verse 3).

I like that spirit. Nathan could have said any one of a thousand things to dampen David's enthusiasm. He might have said, "Why does God need a house? David, don't you understand that God doesn't live in houses?" But Nathan didn't put David down. He helped the dreamer dream his dreams. "Let's go for it."

How far had David's elaborate dream developed before this time? Had he developed blueprints or stockpiled materials for construction? Whatever the case, this dream was born first in David's imagination, or the temple would never have become a reality. Great accomplishments always begin as dreams.

A wistful poet mused:

Man is a dreamer ever,
    He glimpses the hills afar,
And dreams of the things out yonder,
    Where all his tomorrows are.
And back of the sound of the hammer,
    And back of the hissing steam,
And back of the wheels that clamor,
    Is ever a daring dream.
                    — Author unknown

Columbus dreamed a dream and a continent was born. Edison dreamed a dream and night disappeared. Henry Ford dreamed a rolling, rattling dream and put the world on wheels. In the singing brain between his deaf ears, Beethoven dreamed his dreams and put a song in the heart of humanity.

So David dreamed his awesome dream.

God's Desire

Then verse 4: "That night the word of the LORD came to Nathan." Unfortunately, friends often become the bearers of bad news.

Go and tell my servant David, "This is what the LORD says: Are you the one to build me a house to dwell in? I have not dwelt in a house from the day I brought the Israelites up out of Egypt to this day. . . . Wherever I have moved with all the Israelites, did I ever say to any of their rulers whom I commanded to shepherd my people Israel, 'Why do you not build me a house of cedar?' " (verses 5-7)

What an interesting way for God to talk to a man. "It's a nice idea, David. But where in the world did you get it? I didn't say that."

By the way, people all over the place are doing assorted wonderful things "for God"—crackpot ideas which God didn't ask for. Sometimes it is good to seek wise counsel while we are formulating our dreams. We may waste much less time and suffer much less embarrassment.

Are we suggesting David was doing wrong to dream like this? No. Quite the contrary. Years later, when Solomon actually built the temple which David had designed, Solomon explained the Lord's feelings about David's dream:

> The LORD said to my father, David, "Because
> it was in your heart to build a temple for my
> Name, you did well to have this in your heart"
> (2 Chronicles 6:8).

Different Plans

God does not judge us so much by what we achieve as by whom we adore. To dream good dreams may sometimes be even more important than to accomplish them. God didn't bluntly say, "Forget it, David." He said instead, "I have something better for you than what you have going." God loves a dreamer's heart—but He, Himself, often has greater things in mind for us than we could ever have dreamed.

> Tell my servant, David, "This is what the LORD
> Almighty says: Now I will make your name
> great, like the names of the greatest men of the
> earth" (2 Samuel 7:8,9).

"I will give you wonderful things, David, beyond your dreams!"

> When your days are over and you rest with
> your fathers, I will raise up your offspring to
> succeed you, who will come from your own body
> . . . He is the one who will build a house for my
> Name, and I will establish the throne of his
> kingdom forever (2 Samuel 7:12,13).

God was referring here to Solomon, David's son, who was to build, yes, a house. He would also build a kingdom that would last forever. Today no descendant of David or Solomon is sitting on a throne in the Middle East or anywhere else in the world. No continual political entity called the state of Israel has lasted from Solomon's day until now. No, God dreamed of a kingdom of such magnificent proportions and with such unusual dominion that David had no frame of reference with which to comprehend God's promise. Jesus, who is the Son of David, reigns on David's throne, exercising dominion over the entire universe forever. The dream of God completely dwarfed the dream of David.

Had I been David, how would I have felt that day with my dreams dashed? Would I protest, "Why, God? My dream comes from a heart which loves You. I have arrived at a time in my life when I actually could have pulled it off. But now my dream is gone. Why?"

I know some people who have had dreams that God cut off, but then He gave them things beyond their wildest imaginations instead. Bob dreamed since childhood of being an outstanding coach. His career rose meteorically, and at a very young age he was the backfield coordinator of a college football program. He dreamed of being a head coach at that university and was, in fact, considered by many to be next in line for the job. Then things changed swiftly and radically for Bob. The months of bitter disappointment were hard and painful, but Bob would not surrender to that bitterness or turn away from the Lord. God had a different plan for Bob. He is now completing his doctorate, has ministered phenomenally to the staff of a large church, and is dean of the university. In the things for which God is now preparing Bob, his shadow will one day fall over far wider territory and with much more significant impact than it ever would have as a football coach.

Our friends Ed and Georgia planned mission work in Latin America. They spent several years equipping themselves and arranging support partners. They went, but they stayed only briefly, because Georgia became ill with a condition which could not be treated in that country. I'll never forget the week they returned home, crushed and brokenhearted. Then Ed completed his doctorate at Fuller Seminary and now has for some years headed the department of World Missions at Abilene Christian University. God brought them back so He could use them to train missionaries for work on all continents, not just in Latin America.

Carolyn and I dreamed of being missionaries. We spent eleven years trying to do that — and we didn't do it very well. Oh, we left behind us a couple of little churches where we spent eleven years and, by God's grace, some dear friends will be in heaven because of our time in British Columbia.

When we left British Columbia, we dreamed of going to another kind of mission work. The last thing in the world we would have dreamed of was to come to the United States and preach for a large established

Bible-belt church. More than seventeen years have whizzed by since God brought us to this dear church in Abilene, Texas. We didn't want to come here. Then we planned to stay only a short time when we did come. We had not thought of God's using us in this kind of work—but the magnitude of what He has allowed us to be a part of here far surpasses any of our former dreams.

Perhaps as you read these lines, an old ache, nearly forgotten, has risen up again and stabbed your heart as you recall your "what might have been." Few people live a lifetime without some shattered dreams.

God's Redirection

Had I been David when Nathan brought the disappointing news that temple building was not for him, likely I would have slammed shut my briefcase and headed for the door, whining over my shoulder, "Okay, God. I was going to be Your man and I worked my brains out getting all these plans in place. But if You don't like my idea, I'm going home."

Our landscapes are littered with broken, bitter people who are angry with God—and everyone else, too—because their dreams were shattered.

> Let him show a brave face if he can;
>   Let him woo fame and fortune instead;
> But there's little to do but bury a man
>   When the last of his dreams is dead.
>   —William Herbert Carruth

Why should one ever be bitter about redirection when God is the one who chooses the new direction? Does God make bad choices? Isn't God smart enough to know the best use of my life?

Some may be bitter, but not David. No. Look again into his heart as he sat before the Lord and contemplated his shattered dream:

> Who am I, O Sovereign LORD . . . that you have brought me this far? And if this were not enough in your sight, O Sovereign LORD, you have also spoken about the future of the house of your servant" (2 Samuel 7:18,19).

Count the times David repeats those words *Sovereign* and *Lord*. What more can David say to you?

What can I say, God? Why, here I was presuming that my idea would be better than Yours. "According to your will, you have done this great thing and made it known to your servant" (2 Samuel 7:21).

In effect, David is saying, "You have an infinitely better idea than mine, God."

And God is replying, "You bet I do, David." He explains it further to David in 1 Chronicles 22:8-10:

> You are not to build a house for my Name, because you have shed much blood on the earth in my sight. But you will have a son who will be a man of peace and rest. . . . He is the one who will build a house for my Name.

David's Response

God was not, by this, punishing David for the killing which God Himself had commanded him to do. Not at all. Rather, God is saying, "David, some guys have a gift of soldiering and some have a gift of building. I have geared you up to do soldiering and planning—but I designed Solomon to be a ruler and a builder."

After David's dreams were redirected by the Lord, David's attitude could be summarized by these two phrases:

- I am counting my blessings;
- I am praising the Lord.

How great you are, O Sovereign LORD! There is no one like you . . . O LORD Almighty, God of Israel . . . your servant has found courage to offer you this prayer. O Sovereign LORD, you are God. Your words are trustworthy, and you have promised these good things to your servant (2 Samuel 7:22-28).

David's prayer is so different from most of my prayers. Some of mine are screaming protests: "Why did You do this to me, God? Please, gimme what I want. If You won't give it to me, give it to my wife or my kids. At least, bless 'my' church, God."

In contrast, David did not pray a laundry list of wants. He poured out praise and gratitude to God for being the Sovereign Lord of all the earth.

Return with me to the autumn day I stumbled onto those broken dreams at the desolate farmstead. Think. When all of history is consummated, how much time will be spent examining the ruins of that old farmhouse near Putnam, Texas? How long will the disappointed family who abandoned that old house spend mourning their broken dreams?

We really don't have reason to hang around this old world a lot longer, do we? Nothing here actually matters all that much. Can you live with that? The God who sent the prophet Nathan to David with heartbreaking news is the same God who sovereignly rules the affairs of my life and of yours—and the same God whose heart rejoiced in David's words, "O Sovereign LORD," wants to hear those same words from my lips as well.

Oh, sovereign Lord, You are the ruler of heaven and earth and, as our brother Abraham said so many centuries gone by, You are the judge of all the earth, and You will always do right.

With our feeble faith, right now, we try to thank You for our failures and for our broken dreams, because in this painful way You give us hearts which more keenly feel the hurts of others, and which trust You more deeply.

Oh, God, we pray Your word of comfort and hope for those now crushed by broken dreams. Give them a new look at tomorrow.

Father, even when our dreams are shattered and it seems to us You have broken Your promises, give us the courage to delight ourselves in You and to trust You to give us a heart that desires what You desire. In Jesus' name. Amen.

Are you angry with God because
a dream has been shattered?
Remember:
He loves you, and when you give your
disappointment to Him He will comfort
you—and He will give you a new tomorrow.

*One evening David got up from his bed
and walked around on the roof of the palace.
From the roof he saw a woman bathing.
The woman was very beautiful, and
David sent someone to find out about her.
The man said, "Isn't this Bathsheba,
the daughter of Eliam
and the wife of Uriah the Hittite?"
Then David sent messengers to get her.
She came to him, and he slept with her.*
—2 Samuel 11:2-4

*So, if you think you are standing firm,
be careful that you don't fall!*
—1 Corinthians 10:12

EIGHT

David's life underscores four axioms
regarding sexual temptation . . .

Taking the Big Hit

2 Samuel 11

obby collapsed into the blue stuffed chair in the corner of my study and sobbed a long time. Finally, the tortured confession tumbled out. "I'm not sure where it all started. Maybe I watched too many soap operas and began to feel out of things because my life didn't look as glamourous and exciting as the celebrities. Possibly I thought reality would be as free of consequences as *Dynasty* and *Dallas*.

"We worked together, long hours in close proximity . . . And there were a few lingering drinks at a convention . . . I don't know how . . . but it happened. And again. And again. We can't seem to end it. My career is affected. Innocent people are being hurt. My peace of mind is shot. Our affair is leaving a wake of consequences beyond my wildest nightmares."

Bobby — or Bobbie. The name fits either gender; both have made these confessions to me. These could have been David's words as well.

Early one lovely spring evening, while his men were at war, David saw a young woman bathing on her rooftop. No doubt the pleasant scents and sounds of the balmy evening, coupled with the feminine noises as she hummed and splashed in her perfumed bath, cast an overwhelmingly seductive spell.

David saw. He looked again. And what a sight she must have been. Then he scouted — asked about her. "She is married, David. More than that, her husband is one of your famous mighty men, your friend, Uriah, who ate around your campfire and faced death with you during all those dark years in the desert."

David sent for her, anyway, slept with her, and sent her back home. David, why did you do this to me? I trusted you. Why have you let me down? I feel sorry for David, but sometimes I'm angry with him, too.

David's Real Problem

What stream of events brought David to this shameful day? He did not just wake up one balmy spring morning and say, "I have a new idea. Today is the day I will destroy my whole life by committing adultery." His heart was not totally pure at 2 P.M. and then suddenly black at 4.

His adultery was symptomatic of a larger problem which had gradually crept in. Long years of surrender to this weakness, a lustful heart, set him up for the final destructive blow. David dropped a first clue decades earlier: When Abigail, the eloquent, brilliant, beautiful wife of Nabal, came out to meet David, his knees turned to water. Even then, he was a pushover for a skirt. When Nabal died, David's first thought was, "Bring me that woman." Michal's later ego-eroding treatment of David, coupled with their less-than-intimate marriage, may also have helped set him up for this fall.

Most likely, women found David very attractive — he was good looking with "beautiful eyes," and he had a way with words. Once he hit celebrity status, David's lusts were further fueled by the shouts of adoring groupies.

Long before Israel had a king, God charted a threefold test for the office. The king was not to collect an abundance of horses, lest he glory in his power. He was not to amass money, lest he be tempted toward pride and materialism. And, for obvious reasons, he was not to take to himself an abundance of wives (Deuteronomy 17:14*ff.*). David passed the tests of hamstringing captured horses and pouring booty into the treasury (2 Samuel 8:9-11), but he flunked part three. He repeatedly dodged Saul's spear, but out of the darkness came three other deadly lances: money, power and sex. David avoided one and he was grazed by the second, but the third one nailed him through the heart.

A-bomb. That's *A* for adultery.

One woman wasn't enough for David. Besides taking the wives he did in the desert and in Hebron, when he entered the city of Jerusalem he stashed his harem with even more. Then, as now, variety and availability actually increased sexual tensions and appetites. Lust is never satisfied, only inflamed.

In addition to David's appetite being inflamed and his eye being lustful, at the time he met Bathsheba he was particularly vulnerable. He was at midlife.

As I write these lines, I feel a chill. I am fifty years old, the very age David was when he tumbled with Bathsheba. In most centuries men have asked themselves troubling existential questions at midlife. David was accountable to no one. Did he begin, as do many powerful and wealthy midlife men, to think himself above the law? In his popularity, did he begin believing his own press?

David also enjoyed excessive leisure time, relaxing at home in the springtime while others were at war. Sometimes boredom overwhelms and is accentuated by leisure time and luxury. Apparently David was also depressed; he was lying in bed in the middle of the day before he rose to walk around the roof of the palace.

Some pin the rap on Bathsheba, claiming that she seduced David. She should have been more careful about how she dressed, and so should women today, we are told. True. Males are turned on visually. Yes, women of God should select carefully at the dress shop, but the Bible does not indict Bathsheba.

She was simply doing what most women of her time and station did at that time of day. In late afternoon the water in the rooftop rain barrels would be the warmest. Men were usually away from the living quarters then. This was the woman's best hour for bathing. No, the story is not about Bathsheba's seduction, but about David's lustful heart.

Tragic Consequences

A lifetime of vulnerabilities all converged on David that pleasant spring evening that set his passions on fire and overwhelmed his convictions, his better judgment, and his consciousness of God.

Deitrich Bonhoeffer, in his book *Temptation*, says:

> In our members there is a slumbering inclination toward desire which is both sudden and fierce. With irresistible power, desire seizes mastery over the flesh. All at once a secret, smoldering fire is kindled. The flesh burns and is in flames . . . At this moment God is quite unreal to us . . . and only desire for the creature is real . . . Satan does not here fill us with hatred of God, but with forgetfulness of God . . .
>
> The lust thus aroused envelops the mind and will of man in deepest darkness. The powers of clear discrimination and of decision are taken from us.
>
> It is here that everything within me rises up against the Word of God.[1]

David sent for Bathsheba. He slept with her, sinned with her, and sent her back home. His passion spent, David discarded Bathsheba like a used Kleenex. The swirling seductive sequence brought David down. A glance did what Goliath could not do.

This was not the end, however. Although the experience was probably very pleasurable for both David and Bathsheba, Satan is never up front. Any and all consequences are disguised. He didn't mention the lies and deceit that would follow. Or the murder. No mention of the child's death or the havoc in David's family. Satan only said, "Isn't she foxy? And you can have her."

Cover-Up Attempts

She went home, but David kept falling downward. News came that Bathsheba was pregnant. Now David triggered a string of cover-up attempts.

Why did he do anything? He was the king. He was a spiritual leader and a powerful man. There are people who would take advantage of such a position in this kind of situation. From a crassly self-serving perspective, there was no need for David to do anything—but he panicked.

Such is the way of sin. Sin is folly, and it triggers further stupidity.

First, David tried to cover himself with a clumsy attempt at **delusion,** trying to make Bathsheba's husband think that he, Uriah, was the father of the unborn child. *I'll bring Uriah home from the battle to sleep with his wife. Simple.*

Uriah reluctantly answered David's unusual summons. What a charade. David visited warmly with Uriah. "How are things at the battle front? Oh, by the way, since you are in town, why not just go on home and spend the night with your wife?" David closed the door and dusted off his hands thinking, *That's that.* But panic returned the next morning when David found Uriah asleep by the palace door.

Deception came next. *Get him drunk. That's it. When Uriah is drunk, he won't remember for sure what happened in his bedroom.*

Uriah was a better man drunk than David was sober, and again he slept outside David's door. "The ark of God is in the fields, David. Our old buddies from the days in the desert are out there sleeping in the rocks — and dying. I just couldn't feel right in my soft bed at home."

Why didn't something click in David's conscience at this point? But it was not to be. Once the Rubicon is crossed, Satan takes full command. David's panic spun totally out of control.

Then came **destruction**. Oh, David, not your loyal friend! How could you, David?

Next morning David wrote a letter ordering Joab to place Uriah at the front of the battle and then withdraw support, leaving Uriah to die. David, are you putting Uriah's death note in his own hand? You know your awful secret is safe with him. A man like Uriah wouldn't think of betraying your trust and reading the note. Destruction led to disaster. When David knew that Uriah was dead, his next move was incomprehensible. He sent his condolences to Joab by return messenger. "Oh, well, such are the fortunes of war. You lose some; you win some. That's the way it goes."

A-bomb. That's *A* for assassination.

No, David! How could you be that nonchalant? The nerve structure of his conscience had been so traumatized by sin and guilt that he had lost feeling for anything precious. Most of us at some moment in our lives have been dangerously close to that. How could you do this to Uriah? To history? To me? Couldn't you see the consequences? Couldn't your bright mind, your poetic gifts, your God-sensitive soul read the downward spiral and halt it? Lust. Adultery. Hypocrisy. Lies. Drunkenness. Betrayal. Murder. Callousness.

Oh, my David! Oh, my God!

Look this truth in the eye, my friend. Mark it down for the centuries: Most adulterers, at some moment, have considered the death of someone. *Things sure would be better if my mate were dead and I could have my lover;* or, *If this forbidden lover, whom I cannot resist, would be dead, this thing would be over with;* or, *I wish I could die and be out of this;* or more commonly, *We'll murder the unborn child and thus escape the consequences.* These are murderous thoughts. David is not alone. Not alone.

Consequences rolled in — wave upon wave — leaving both guilty and innocent awash.

David's child died.

David's influence was destroyed.

David's family disintegrated. The sword hung over his house as brother raped sister and brother slaughtered brother. His kingdom fell into shambles.

Three thousand years later people abuse this story every day. David's has become the classic rationalization for believers who plunge into sexual sin. The story cuts both ways. David sounds a warning to those tempted, but chaste. Ironically, however, to the sexually undisciplined, he becomes an excuse. Such is the way of the most sacred truths of heaven — easily distorted. Again we can see that the heart of the individual person is the key. Listen: The point of David's message is not justification, but disaster. The fallout is horrendous.

Four Axioms

The dark demise of David underscores four heavyweight axioms.

First, *adultery is always wrong*. Never right. Never helpful. Never excusable. Never overlooked by God. Wrong.

Second, *adultery is always ruinous*. Today our media glamorizes adultery, making sexual promiscuity seem essential to fully free and fulfilled personhood. Yet, hear the unanimous testimony of those who know the score and have experienced the tragedy: Adultery is never, ever, without destructive consequences. It is always ruinous. *Dallas* and *Dynasty* lie. Real-life episodes do not end with a quip, a smile, and a commercial break. In reality the sadness goes on, and on.

What if no one ever knows? Adultery still erodes the heart. Even friends who don't know what is going on in your bedroom suffer. While a person lives in this duplicity, subtle signals in his life steer even innocent friends away from confrontation with God. The adulterer cannot bear to face God. He dodges from spiritual resources, thus influencing the tone of his circle of relationships, subtly leading the whole away from God, not toward Him.

For the offender himself, this sin exacts an enormous toll. Internal upheaval and stress consume emotional energies. Deceit leads toward double identity which can be described only as a pathology—a sort of schizophrenia that eventually totally erodes the character and sometimes the sanity.

The environment becomes flooded with lies which breed further mistrust and confusion. Hurt, anger, shame and brokenheartedness batter those who are close to the adulterer: the mate and the children, and trusting, respecting, loving friends.

The consequences of adultery also alter personalities and pierce even to the heart.

> Flee from sexual immorality. All other sins a man commits are outside his body, but he who sins sexually sins against his own body (1 Corinthians 6:18).

Always ruinous. No wonder the Bible says:

> Do not be deceived: Neither the sexually immoral nor idolators nor adulterers nor male prostitutes nor homosexual offenders will inherit the kingdom of God (1 Corinthians 6:9,10).

Third, *We must always run from adultery.* Sexual temptation cannot be successfully dealt with except by running from it.

Again Bonhoeffer warns:

> Therefore, the Bible teaches us in times of temptation in the flesh to *flee*: "Flee fornication" (1 Corinthians 6:18). "Flee from idolatry" (1 Corinthians 10:14). "Flee youthful lusts" (2 Timothy 2:22). "Flee the lust of the world" ([see] 2 Peter 1:4). There is no resistance to Satan other than flight (All KJV).[2]

Dear reader, you know and I know, from experience, that these words from Bonhoeffer and the Bible are true. David did not flee. He fell.

Running means there are some things to *run away* from.

🔱 Run Away

Run away from the temptation to adultery. Keep the heart pure. Stand close guard on the gates which lead to your thoughts and imaginations. Books. Conversation. Media. Movies. Pictures. Music. Some of these we need to run from. If this sounds tough and arbitrary, remember how straight Jesus talked:

> I tell you that anyone who looks at a woman lustfully has already committed adultery with her in his heart. If your right eye causes you to sin, gouge it out and throw it away. It is bet-ter for you to lose one part of your body than for your whole body to be thrown into hell
> (Matthew 5:28,29).

Jesus! Could you possibly mean that? Are you really saying it is better to be physically maimed than sexually impure?

Run from our own points of vulnerability and steer around them. What moods find me most vulnerable? What situations? What persons could most likely get to me? I had best identify them and write them down, and plan safe alternatives in their places.

Fleeing may also mean running away from a specific person. Joseph handled the woman who had the hots for him by physically running out of the place. She grabbed his coat, but he split so fast he left his empty garment in her hand. Dare I linger when Joseph had to skedaddle?

Did someone just say, "But I trust the Lord. I don't need all these human checks and balances"?

Placing ourselves next to disastrous temptation is not the walk of spiritual giants, but the path of fools. Get away! With that certain person who lights your fire, stay out of empty apartments, secluded coves and back seats. Stay away. Even if this means confessing these vulnerabilities to certain stable, spiritual advisors and making yourself accountable to them.

When you find yourself in a situation you cannot handle, no matter how ridiculous your exit may look, get out of there as fast as your feet will carry you.

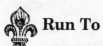 **Run To**

Fleeing also means *running to* someone.

Run to Jesus. He promised to strengthen us "through his spirit in [our] inner being" (Ephesians 3:16). "Put ye on the Lord Jesus Christ, and make not provision for the flesh" (Romans 13:14, KJV). That is spiritual maturity. He has made a promise:

> God is faithful; he will not let you be tempted
> beyond what you can bear. But when you are
> tempted, he will also provide a way out
> (1 Corinthians 10:13).

Run to the people of Jesus, too. When I am on the road and in a lonely city, if possible, I make myself accountable to Christian friends in that place. There have been times when I have called Carolyn and asked her to jump on the next plane, bus, or mule train to come to where I was. I don't trust myself. I don't trust you either! But in the Holy Spirit, we have the power to say no and to flee. The Spirit often works through people. I choose often to run to accountability, because I know that otherwise disaster would surely befall me.

This is the only way I'll ever stay straight, and it's the only way you will, too.

"Childish!" you say? No, spiritual maturity.

The **fourth** axiom is: *We must repent of adultery.* "For me it is too late," you may say. "I have fallen already." The message is the same. If you have fallen, get up and repent.

David said, "I have sinned." He didn't just say it with his lips. He said it with everything in his life. Repent. Immediately, openly, completely repent. Flee and repent. Of course God will forgive.

> And . . . some of you were [adulterers]. But you were washed, you were sanctified, you were justified in the name of the Lord Jesus Christ (1 Corinthians 6:11).

The story of David and Bathsheba is not about sin, but about God. The God with the broken heart always waits to forgive.

We all deserve to die, adultery or no — but if we repent, He will forgive. If you are in this sin, confess completely and freely to God and to some person you trust. Then break off every contact you may have, in any way, with the person who would tempt you.

Listen. Every Christian walks with a limp. Each of us has at least one area of vulnerability. All of us have dark chapters we hope God can forget, because we surely can't. We operate each day only on the grace and goodness of God. We all need Him so badly.

Some of God's greatest ministry is done by those who walk with a limp. Remember: David was God's man before Bathsheba and Uriah. Afterward he was still God's man—and his sin was no worse than yours or mine. David bore the scars of his sin, but in the Healer's hands, those scars give help to the ages.

Don Francisco sings:

I loved you long before the time
your eyes first saw the day,
And everything I've done has been
to help you on your way.
But you took all you wanted,
then at last you took your leave
And traded off your kingdom
for the lies that you believed.
Even though my name's been splattered
by the mire in which you lie,
I'd take you back this instant
if you'd come to me and cry.

* * * * *

I don't care where you've been sleepin',
I don't care who made your bed,
I already gave my life to set you free.
There's no sin you can imagine
that is stronger than my love,
And it's all yours
if you'll come home again with me.[3]

Have you been or are you now
dangerously close to insensitivity toward
the perils of sexual temptation?
Remember:
Repentance and confession
always brings God's forgiveness.

Better is open rebuke
than hidden love.
Wounds from a friend can be trusted,
but an enemy multiplies kisses.
— Proverbs 27:5,6

Brothers, if someone is caught in a sin,
you who are spiritual should restore him gently.
But watch yourself, or you also may be tempted.
Carry each other's burdens,
and in this way you will
fulfill the law of Christ.
— Galatians 6:1,2

NINE

*Nathan demonstrates five requisites
for an effective approach . . .*

Caring Enough
to Confront

2 Samuel 12

 was blasted out of my sleep, that morning in 1988, by rude sounds and bad lyrics from the NBC *Today* show. The song was a musical spoof, which ended with the words: "For the future of our nation, just rub your crystal ball."

Media figures had a field day with Donald Regan's "kiss and tell" book, *For the Record*. The impression was that the current chief advisor in the White House was actually Nancy Reagan's astrologer. The American public joined in the laughter. Behind the amusement, however, some observers registered alarm. Would President Reagan actually depend on such an advisor? Is it possible that the leader of the most powerful nation in the world would make decisions of global proportions on the advice of a "smoke and mirrors" quack?

Three thousand years ago the leader of the most powerful nation in the world definitely made some major decisions on the word of a strange advisor. King David had his own inside man named Nathan.

This consultant was no back-street wizard with a crystal ball, though. Nathan was an open-faced friend of David, who kept popping up and confronting the king with disturbing facts. Nathan was willing to cross David when no one else would. Likely others heard whisperings; some even may have known facts. Yet only Nathan told David the brutal truth.

Our day, too, could use some courage. What is our responsibility when someone we dearly love and respect is deep into sin? There are wrong things to do. One is to ignore the issue, hope it's not true, pretend it won't be discovered, or hope it will go away. This approach leads to continuing deterioration of the person in sin. Or friends may talk *about*, not *to* the sinner. They illustrate the "memory verse" attempted by a Sunday school child: "Go into all the world and preach the 'gossip' to every creature." Disaster compounds in every direction when this option is exercised.

Nathan followed a third option: the way of loving confrontation. All Scripture confirms his approach. The plan of action is clear:

> Brothers, if someone is caught in sin, you who
> are spiritual should restore him gently. But
> watch yourself, or you also may be tempted
> (Galatians 6:1).

"But," someone objects, "Jesus warned that we should not judge!" Jesus referred here to the assigning of motives, not to the confronting of destructive behavior. He said we should not pretend to know what is in the heart of another. Only God knows that.

Motive-assigning is very different from loving confrontation because of open sinful behavior. Wickedness subtly seduces us and blinds us so that we may become oblivious to our own sin, which is obvious to those around us. Often our only hope is that someone will lovingly confront us. Solomon said: "Wounds from a friend can be trusted, but an enemy multiplies kisses" (Proverbs 27:5,6). In this spirit, Nathan confronted his powerful friend David.

A Time Interval

David's cover-up appeared for some time to be successful. The Bible bridges that time with eight simple words: "The thing David had done displeased the LORD" (2 Samuel 11:27).

Meanwhile, a "love child" had been born to David and Bathsheba, a child to whom David became deeply attached. David assumed the whole incident was effectively hidden from the eyes of Israel. No scandal broke across the kingdom. No consequences resulted that year.

When David took Bathsheba to be his wife, he no doubt rose in public opinion poles. "Such a wonderful man. Poor Uriah fell in battle, likely without enough life insurance, but David cares for that poor widow like one of his wives and treats that child as his own." Three knew differently, however. One was David. One was Bathsheba. The third was God. And God was waiting.

About a year after the adulterous rendezvous, like a bolt of lightning from a clear blue sky, God sent Nathan to confront David.

Why wait a year? In the first blush of infatuation, excitement blots out rationality. To approach David during that time may have been as helpful as trying to reason with an alcoholic while he is drunk. Time had to elapse for David's head to clear. Let him find Bathsheba's nylons soaking in the sink and give him a year of mornings across the breakfast table from her.

David also needed time to come to terms with the tempest in his own heart. A year of sleepless nights must have found David often staring into the darkness, haunted by Uriah's ghost. What would conscience do to David, with Uriah's face pictured in those treacherous final moments when he realized his friend had done him in? Perhaps for a year David had imagined the soft eyes of his children rejecting him like a foreign object.

What of the awful hours David sat in the dark under the penetrating eyes of a broken-hearted heavenly Father? "When I kept silent, my bones wasted away," David said. God had left David impaled on guilt, with no relief, for a year: ". . . through my groaning all day long" (Psalm 32:3). Possibly some mornings David rose feeling better about himself—till he looked in the mirror, and then groans from the depths of his heart would roll from his throat. "For day and night your hand was heavy upon me" (verse 4), till the day God's time was right, and Nathan strode purposefully into the palace.

Nathan's Confrontation

David had amply demonstrated his violent side, and he had merely to raise a finger for Nathan's head to roll, yet Nathan confronted David without batting an eye. His technique was delicately indirect. He told an irresistible story. "A poor man owned but one pet lamb which he loved, holding it in his arms and hand-feeding it like a child. Across the road lived a wealthy rancher with thousands of sheep. Yet when the rich man threw a barbecue for his out-of-town guests, rather than roasting a ram from his own huge flocks, he slaughtered the poor neighbor's pet. What should be done to him, David?"

You could have scraped David off the ceiling! "The man deserves to die," he roared. "At least make him repay four times over." Surely before these words cleared David's lips, things must have registered.

Four times, David? Interesting. David took one life from Uriah, but before God was finished, four of David's own sons died. David was sentenced by his own lips.

How long did Nathan wait before unveiling his next line? See how his fingers trembled as he stared sadly into the eyes of the man he had so long admired. How carefully Nathan reached for the words which cut the air so clearly that they still ring across the centuries. "David, oh David, you are the man." Thus, Nathan deftly pierced David's conscience.

What tears must have tumbled down Nathan's twitching cheeks as he delivered God's words like hammer blows. Yet Nathan was merely a conduit for the tears which flowed from the broken heart of God:

> I anointed you king over Israel . . . delivered
> you from the hand of Saul . . . gave your
> master's house to you, and your master's wives
> into your arms . . . if all this had been too little,

I would have given you even more. Why did
you despise the word of the LORD by doing
what is evil in his eyes? (2 Samuel 12:7-9)

Then, simply, eloquently, poignantly, David
said the only fitting thing he could say at that moment:
"I have sinned" (verse 13).

David's Psalm of Confession

Later David would write down his confession
for every guilt-ridden soul to share:

Have mercy on me, O God,
according to your unfailing love . . .
blot out my transgressions.
Wash away all my iniquity
and cleanse me from my sin (Psalm 51:1,2).

The title above this psalm says these words
were written after Nathan's painful visit. They bear the
soul scars of a man living the rest of his days with the
fruit of his folly:

. . . my sin is always before me.
Against you, you only, have I sinned
and done what is evil in your sight
(Psalm 51:3,4).

His words still ring true. A few weeks ago, I
went back and touched base with a half-dozen men who
in the last three years have confessed to me they committed adultery against their wives. Each of these men
happens to be a minister of the gospel.

I asked the six: If you could write these lines
and be totally open about what went down in your life,
what advice would you give?

In one way or another, these men all said, "Tell them that 'my sin is always before me.' I believe God has forgiven me, but I have difficulty forgiving myself. My self-respect is shot. I see suspicion and resentment in everyone's eyes." David, no doubt, also felt accusing eyes everywhere, but he knew his real sin was against God. No matter how well we keep secrets, God knows and God grieves. So David prayed:

> Create in me a pure heart . . .
> Restore to me the joy of your salvation . . .
>   let the bones which you have crushed rejoice
>   (Psalm 51:10,12,8).

"Help me forget," I hear David pleading, "and give me back my emotional health."

Nathan jumped on David's genuine confession, "The LORD has taken away your sin" (2 Samuel 12:13). What good news! This is what God always waits to do. "You are not going to die!"

According to the law, David deserved to die — but Nathan said, "You won't die." That's God's *grace.*

Yet sin carries consequences: "The son born to you will die." That's God's *judgment.*

David's child lay sick for a while. David sat on the ground grieving, sleepless by night, not eating by day. Then the child died. So David got up, showered, ate breakfast and went to the office — forgiven.

This recovery might never have happened if his friend Nathan had not mustered the courage to confront him. Love at times demands that we confront. We have all heard someone admit, "Oh, yeah, I knew he was doing that for two years." Then why, in the name of God, didn't you say something to him?

"I didn't think it was any of my business."
You are his brother, are you not? Or his sister?

For Effective Confronting

Confronting is not fun, nor is it easy. But
learn to do it we must, and here is where Nathan offers
some helpful insights.

First: TRUTH. The wayward person is to be
approached with biblical truth, not with our own preju-
dices. A young stranger was confronted by an older
deacon in one of our church washrooms because the
young man's hair was "too long" and he wore sandals.
We are not talking about that kind of confrontation—a
matter of opinion, not of truth. Only when clear biblical
teaching is being violated is confrontation called for.

We must confront only when we know the
truth, the real facts about another's behavior. Scripture
says, "Do not entertain an accusation . . . unless it is
brought by two or three witnesses" (1 Timothy 5:19).

"Just the facts," warns Paul, "not mere hear-
say." Not gossip. Not suspicion. Only facts. Thoughtful
people have discovered that solid facts are difficult to
come by. Only through long, patient interest in a brother or sister will we really know whether our information
is factual. Only love will invest that kind of energy.
Then we must use those facts only on behalf of the loved
one, to clear up gossip or to confront sin.

In addition, a helpful confrontation can grow
only out of true motives. Paul said we should go to our
brother overtaken in a fault, but only "in a spirit of
gentleness, looking to your own heart" (see Galatians
6:1).

The tough question is, Why am I doing this? Do I have a right to do it? The only right we have is a love running deep enough that we come with a broken heart, wanting to see a life change. If we confront out of one-upmanship or vengeance, we will do only harm and are not fit to confront.

TRUTH. Biblical truth. Facts. True motives.

Second, TIMING. Nathan waited until God sent him, because David simply wasn't rational before God's time. I asked our half-dozen adultery-scarred friends, "What was helpful and what was not helpful when people attempted to reach out to you?"

One answered, "Some were not helpful at all — they rushed in like fools where angels fear to tread."

Another continued, "There were some, however, who had put their lives down beside me. They already held a track record of concern. So what they said to me I had to listen to. But," he added, "there was a period of time when I wasn't listening to anything because the time was not right — I was not ready."

God's timing is crucial. Far better to wait a little too long, than to jump in too soon.

Third, TACT. Nathan skillfully worded a story which was designed to penetrate David's defenses and invade his heart. We dare not shoot from the hip at such a delicate and skittish target as a wayward soul. At times I have actually written out the exact words I wanted to say and then sat down in front of the friend and read what I had written. Anything as priceless as another person deserves prayerful thought and all the creative tact that can be mustered.

The **fourth** word is COURAGE. When Nath-
an stepped into David's palace, intent on confrontation,
not only did he risk his life as mentioned earlier, but he
also risked a long friendship. Confrontation is most
effective when we are risking a long friendship. If I am
not risking a friendship, if I have not earned credibility
with that person, I should let someone else do the
confronting.

Even then the person approaching may be
rejected. A person on the defensive may easily mis-
construe motives. Concern may look like an attack,
occasionally stirring such defenses that this person may
break off the relationship. Such is the risk. Even if the
person responds and is healed, he may avoid us in the
future because our presence reminds him of old hurts.

Repeat: *Confronting risks friendships and it
takes rock-ribbed courage.*

Finally: HOPE. There is no use confronting
a person unless he is pointed to Jesus, to hope, to
forgiveness. If I am personally hurt by my own sin, such
is justice. Even if my sin deeply violates someone I love,
this is still not the central issue and doesn't compare to
the fact that my sin has offended the holiness and
broken the heart of almighty God.

Scare Tactics

My friend Tom Olbricht tells about pigeons
roosting on the wires over his uncle's used car lot. To
keep the pigeons from spatter-painting the cars, Tom
and his brother declared war with their .22 caliber
rifles. The ammunition was expensive and the pigeon
supply was unlimited, so the boys soon decided their
method wasn't cost effective. No matter. They devised

a better plan. They noticed that each time a poor victim fell, the bang of the .22 had scared off all the other pigeons. So the boys switched to blanks, which worked just as well at far less expense.

However, before long the pigeons caught on. They noticed that when the boys fired blanks, no pigeons fell. Gradually the pigeons became accustomed to the sound and ignored it. Now the really serious problem presented itself. Tom and his brother switched back to live ammunition, but it was too late. Even the live ammunition did not frighten the pigeons. The .22 rifle would crack and one of the pigeons would topple dead from the wire, while his closest companions would hang tough and merely cock their heads to watch their buddy fall. Now the pigeons really came home to roost in flocks, and nothing could be done about it, as the pigeons had no fear, even of live ammunition!

Something like this happens to people when preachers and parents and policemen attempt to manipulate behavior by scare tactics, rather than by God-centered conviction.

This traditional scare-tactic approach specifically applied to sexual behavior goes something like this: "If you fool around, any or all of three bad things can happen: (1) someone is liable to get pregnant; or (2) you might get a disease; or (3) your reputation will be damaged." Later, along came the pill and neutered the first argument. Penicillin fixed the second one. When times changed so that sexual experience actually enhanced the reputation, argument number three was turned inside out.

This approach to morality didn't work any more because, until the AIDS scare, the fear factor had lost its clout. Besides, it was built on bad theology—it appealed, not to God's holiness, but to self-protection.

On the other hand, David said the word *God*. "God, my sin was against You!" David did not say, "Look what I did to Bathsheba, to Uriah, to my family, to the kingdom, to myself, to three thousand years of history." He said, "*God,* I sinned against You and You only. So I'm bringing *You* a broken heart." We must understand that our sins are against God, so that when God forgives, the forgiveness is real no matter how others treat us. It is God who "so loved us that He gave . . . " God does not record our progress in a book to see how long we maintain our performance record before He trusts us. He knows when our hearts are genuine and He forgives.

 One Ending

Truth. Timing. Tact. Courage. Hope.

Where will all of this lead? Confrontation can end in one of two ways. Most of the time, when we muster the courage to confront, we will not lose a friend. The few times I have risked confronting a beloved friend over serious sins in his or her life, far from becoming enemies, we now have deeper trust and deeper respect for each other. And I think more, not less, of the people who have loved me enough to painfully confront me. I know these people really care, because they have invested value into my life.

Such was the case with Nathan and David. In fact, when David and Bathsheba's third child was born, David named him Nathan. Imagine. After that painful confrontation, rather than resenting the prophet, David actually named one of his sons for Nathan.

The Other Ending

However, not all confrontation stories end this well. Remember, Saul was confronted, too—by Samuel.

Charles Swindoll tells the story of a well-known minister and his son who worked together in evangelism. Their ministry flourished until his son became suspicious that his father was spending too much time with a certain young woman. The son finally confronted his father. At first the father stonewalled him and angrily denied. The son backed off respectfully, watching and praying for some months. His suspicions grew, though, and he finally became convinced the gossip about his father was true.

Then one day the son took his father for a drive on a country road. He stopped the car and again confronted his father. In essence he said, "Dad, I am not suspicious anymore. I know now what is going on between you and this young woman."

Again the father angrily denied all the son's charges, until the son said, "Dad, right there in the glove compartment is a tape, recorded while you and that girl thought you were alone. I will play the tape if you want me to."

They drove home in silence. The father packed his bags and moved in with the girl, thus shattering his ministry, his marriage, and the hearts of the people who loved him.[1]

The Human Heart Factor

There is no guarantee that loving confrontation will always be effective, because of a variable over which no one has control except the person directly involved. That variable factor is the human heart.

As you read this book, you may be agonizing over something that has gone wrong in your life. You desperately want it resolved, but you cannot find the courage to say anything. Since no one but you knows, there is no Nathan to confront you. Maybe the Holy Spirit is confronting you this very moment, through me.

Or possibly you know something sinful in the life of a beloved brother or sister. You have known it for some time, but you felt it was none of your business, or you lacked courage, or you did not know what to do. Let these lines say to you: Before God, care enough to confront. Without Nathan, David may well have died unrepentant. Yet through loving confrontation, God made David a forgiven man, a man after the heart of God, a man who would still wear a crown and sing his songs of worship.

Long live Nathan!

When you need to confront someone,
and you fear the risk,
Remember:
The Holy Spirit can give you
the wisdom to do it lovingly
and the courage to care enough.

They sow the wind,
and reap the whirlwind.
—Hosea 8:7

TEN

*David's lifestyle influenced his family the same
as ours does . . .*

Families
in the
Fast Lane

2 Samuel 13–19

 y father warned me of a certain phe-
nomenon years ago. When our chil-
dren first came along, I often asked
Dad for advice on child-rearing.
"Dad," I would say, "help me. How did
you build the healthy relationship we
have with each other? What should I
do to assure this with my children?"

Dad always answered, "I can't help you. I
reared you in another setting and at a different time.
Your kids are growing up in a new and rapidly changing

153

world, and they face pressures you never experienced. Parenting for you, son, will be far more difficult than it was for me."

A Common Drama

A common drama repeatedly plays itself out in my study. The plot remains constant, although the characters change. *Scene one* goes something like this: A student sits across the desk from me. "My parents don't seem to understand me. But then I don't know why my parents prize the things they do, either. I guess I need to find their roots."

Scene two: Enter parent. "My kids! I don't understand them at all." The parent may have grown up in a world where life was well ordered. Back in those times, roots ran deep and values stood clear. People knew what they valued and the whole town more or less reinforced good morals and stable lifestyles. Then the communities were linked by urban sprawl; Mom and Dad soon found themselves rolling down the freeways in big cosmopolitan cities, where they are now raising their children. The children were born away from the stable roots and sterling values of the parents.

Families in the fast lane.

David and Absalom were like this. David was born to the Bethlehem pasture. His roots ran deeply through the soil around Bethlehem and into the God of his fathers. He learned early to sing the Hebrew songs and prize the ancient values. When he was catapulted from the back pasture to the front page, firm values gave direction to his life. When he wandered, as he often did, he knew his roots and he was always drawn back.

David's son Absalom, however, was born in a palace. He didn't know his father's roots. David, in a world packed with pressure and action, did not take time to help his son find the ancient Hebrew ways. No invisible infrastructure held Absalom's life stable. As a result, David and Absalom seemed to live on different planets. The tragic result is known to the ages.

A family in the fast lane.

Reaping the Whirlwind

After his sin with Bathsheba and the murder of his friend Uriah, David repented and God forgave him. However, the consequences of sin often continue long after forgiveness has been granted. "Sowing to the wind means reaping the whirlwind." Fathers and sons. Roots and freeways. David and Absalom. David sowed the wind and in his son, he reaped the whirlwind.

First, the whirlwind brought rape. Amnon, son of David, fell in lust with his half sister Tamar. Amnon's buddy conned David into inadvertently helping Amnon get to Tamar. As Amnon feigned illness, David sent word to Tamar to "go to the house of your brother Amnon and prepare some food for him."

Poor David, how out of touch he was. When Tamar arrived with the food, Amnon raped her and, with his passion spent, "he hated her more than he had loved her" (2 Samuel 13:15). He sent Tamar out and bolted the door.

David was furious. So, David, you are only furious? But what else could David do? Where did Amnon get that look in his eye? Could he have been imitating the look in his father's eye? How does David punish a boy for taking a page out of Daddy's own book? David was furious! Indeed!

Absalom was furious, too—Tamar was his full sister—but Absalom's fury had purposeful teeth in it. For two years his hatred for Amnon festered as Absalom watched for an opportune moment. Then rape begot revenge. Absalom casually invited David to come along on a family sheepshearing. David declined, blind to his son's murderous intentions. So the boys went without their dad. Meanwhile, Absalom gathered his men and instructed them in treachery. "We will get Amnon drunk."

Oh, David, where have we heard this before? Who got Uriah drunk?

"When he is drunk," plotted Absalom, "fall on him and kill him." *Deja vu!* Another page from Daddy's bloody book!

Murder. Brother against brother. Poor David. How he grieved. He was paralyzed by his own guilt. Yes, David was "grieved." That's all. Big deal.

Reaction to Parents' Indifference

Absalom hid in Geshur with his grandfather for three years, during which time David made no attempt to bring his son home. Finally, after those three years, David brought Absalom back to Jerusalem, but, incredibly, even then David said, "He must go to his own house" (2 Samuel 14:24). So for two more years Absalom did not see his father's face.

The opposite of love is not hatred; it is indifference. Whether he meant to or not, David was communicating the opposite of love for Absalom.

True, all this time David was crying over his son, but Absalom didn't see his father's tears. David's pride stood in the way. Or was it insecurity? What convoluted thoughts tortured David's mind?

Through all this, Absalom wanted to be with his father. Did he have mixed feelings, too? What son really wants to be rejected by his own dad? Absalom pleaded with Joab, "Help me get an audience with my father." When Joab ignored the appeal, Absalom set Joab's field on fire.

Kids still do this. When children are ignored too long by parents, they will "set some fields on fire." The fire may fall in a variety of ways. I sat on the back porch of a Tennessee farmhouse as a sweet little girl told me she was trying to get pregnant to gain her parents' attention. Another young lady of whom I know deliberately led her mother to overhear a telephone conversation in which the girl boasted to a friend about her sexual exploits with the guys at school. The exploits were imaginary, but they did set the fields on fire.

Other kids try booze or drugs, or they even attempt suicide, desperately calling for a relationship with distanced parents. Yet like Absalom, they are often left out of the parents' emotional loop. A father may even be with his children for years physically without the children ever really seeing his face—only the reflection of it in the mirror of the TV set.

According to *U. S. News & World Report,*[1] 53 percent of teenagers report spending less than thirty minutes a day with their fathers, and 45 percent of teenagers report spending less than thirty minutes a day with their mothers.

Of 1,000 teenagers interviewed, 25 percent do not discuss their daily activities with their parents, 42 percent had not received parental words of praise during the past twenty-four hours, 50 percent had not gotten a hug or kiss, 54 percent had not heard the words, "I love you," and 79 percent said they had not been helped with homework by a parent.[2]

More Whirlwind Fallout

Rape! Revenge! Revolt! David's sky continued to rain fallout from his horrendous sins. Violence escalated as Absalom actually plotted the death of his own father. He cleverly won the hearts of the people by sitting at the gates, shaking hands, kissing babies, making lavish "campaign promises," and grabbing the power. Finally, Absalom made his open and decisive move to kill David and seize the throne in Jerusalem.

Terrifying news reached David's ears: "The hearts of the men of Israel are with Absalom" (2 Samuel 15:13).

David responded, "Come! We must flee, or none of us will escape from Absalom" (verse 14).

Child revolt now has the parent on the run.

Beecher and Beecher, a husband-wife team, have written a book entitled *Parents on the Run*. They suggest that "the adult-centered home of yesteryear made parents masters and children slaves. The child-centered home of today, however, has made the parents the slaves and the children the masters."[3]

Master. Slave. Absalom became both.

A father's sins had led to rape, then revenge, revolt, and even repulsiveness.

Absalom pitched a tent on the palace roof and had sexual intercourse with his father's wives "in the sight of all Israel." In the ancient world, the conqueror often ravaged the wives of the conquered as a statement of total domination. This accounts in part for Absalom's repulsive actions, but a significant addition to the ritual makes this act an eloquent mockery. "The roof" was where David had lusted after Bathsheba and fetched her for adultery; so, cryptically, Absalom violated David's wives on "the roof." Another dreadful page torn from the father's book!

As David fled Jerusalem, "the whole countryside wept aloud" (2 Samuel 15:23). David, with his eyes scarcely visible under the cloak thrown over his bowed head, stumbled blindly up the steep, the whiteness of his bared feet splotched with blood, his body convulsed in sobs (verse 30, "weeping as he went").

The people around him were wailing, too, but for different reasons. David cried over a lost boy—the people wept over a lost kingdom.

David's family was running completely out of control in the fast lane.

In the Systems School of Family Therapy, researchers talk of "genograms," which trace patterns within family systems from generation to generation. The foibles of the parents repeat themselves in the children with alarming regularity. This certainly rang true for David.

From rape and revenge through revolt to repulsiveness. All led to enormous regrets. Down they go. Families in the fast lane. Absalom attacked David and his armies. David sent his troops out to repel the attack, but with strange orders. As the lines of fierce armed men marched out the gates of Mahanaim, I can see David grab the arm and look into the eyes of each officer pleading, "Be careful for my son. Win the battle, but please be careful. He is my boy." As the rear of the army slipped out of sight over the horizon, did David whisper one more time, "Oh, please, please, be careful with my son"?

But soldiers are not trained to be careful. Absalom fled defeated that day, and a low-hanging limb snagged his hair. Joab, the tough and wily general, ruthlessly ran him through with darts, and Absalom died on the spot. Messengers ran to David and bluntly reported, "I wish all of your enemies were as dead as Absalom."

Poor David. Disaster in the fast lane. Stumbling up the stairs under the weight of his sorrow. Agony. Tears. Grief over his dead son. But even more grief over the regrets of a guilty father. "Oh, Absalom, my son. Why couldn't it have been me rather than you?" (See 18:33).

We reluctantly leave the scene for now. In the next chapter we shall attempt to bring some comfort to parents in pain. First, let us backtrack and review: How did David get here? We must know so we don't wind up here ourselves.

Ramp to the Fast Lane

David's sad end is likely not attributable to one sin alone but to the style of his life once he entered the fast lane.

To begin with, David was out of sight. He was seldom at home. Too many battles. Too many responsibilities. Too many wives. Too many children. How could intimacy flourish?

Too many soldiers to keep track of, too many construction projects, too much money to count. Too many preoccupations. David was the classic absentee father.

In 1984, *Newsweek*[4] magazine reported on the life and death of Frederick Flicks. This wealthy West German industrialist amassed a personal fortune of more than 1.5 billion dollars. At the time of his death, his companies annually generated 3 billion dollars plus. But *Newsweek* reported that Flicks had "one very human weakness." He could control billions of dollars, but he could not control his family. The lives of his children were all disasters. Apparently, he even lost sight of his wife's personhood. When Flicks's wife died, the day of her funeral she was buried at 3 P.M., and he was back in the office by 5.

Flicks's tragedy is not unique. In one form or another it occurs in families of many businessmen, athletes, other celebrities, politicians and even preachers. Reaping the whirlwind. Absentee father. Fast lane. Out of sight. No time right now. Someone else will nurture "roots." The Sunday school teacher. The youth minister.

"What's that? Of course, I love you. Why else would I have given you that BMW? I am eager to send you to the best schools; nothing is too good for you. Be an achiever, boy, a winner."

Dad is anchored by his roots, but the son's roots end at the hard surface of the freeway, because Dad is out of sight.

Out of Touch

David didn't know his boys. When a father is out of sight, inevitably he will drift out of touch. He didn't know Amnon. He didn't seem to see in Amnon's eye the lustful look which had once been his own. He was out of touch with Absalom, too, oblivious to the murderous expression on his face. For two years Absalom plotted revenge against his brother right under David's nose. Not only was David out of touch by being out of sight, but he also was out of touch emotionally. Absalom, the wayward son, was allowed to live in the same town with his father for years but not allowed to see his father's face. How out of touch! Tears over his stranger-son. Pride. Insecurity. Confusion. Emotional distance.

Roger Rosenblatt, in *Time* magazine, October 6, 1986, starkly stated, "Little murders are committed daily in homes where Mom and Dad sit planted in front of pieces of paper or the Cosby show, while the children lie still as dolls on their beds and gaze at ceiling fixtures . . . See how free everybody is. The only things missing are the essentials: authority, responsibility, attention and love . . . Between the parent and child there is a monsterlike silence. The freedom children seek is the freedom from silence. The freedom they are given too often is the freedom of the damned."[5]

For all their geographic proximity, too many dads are out of touch with their children.

⚜ Out of Line

David was not only out of sight and out of touch, but he was also way out of line. Treacherous murder to cover adultery. David was big-time, heavy-duty out of line.

Kids suffer when parents are out of line. The tragic reality is that, even though kids may be angry at their parents' sins, kids often imitate, and magnify, with a vengeance, the very patterns they have hated in their parents, whether it be workaholism, alcoholism, affairs, or divorce.

My secretary nervously interrupted a no-phone-calls-accepted hour. "You have got to take this one," she said.

The caller instantly grabbed my attention. "Sir," he mumbled, "would you please pray with me? I am waiting for my mother and her boyfriend to come home. When they walk through the door, I am going to blow them away with this loaded rifle. Then I will blow myself away. Please pray for me. They are due any minute."

After a long, tense conversation I was able to persuade the young man that I should come to his house and pray with him.

When I walked in his door, he was indeed clutching a loaded and cocked 30.06 in his crippled hand. As he tried to shake hands with me, he dragged its muzzle across my belt buckle. In an agitated and drug-addled state of mind, he poured out his story, which included child abuse from the time of his earliest memory. His mother had lived with an endless series of boyfriends. Once he remembered being locked for days in a travel trailer. His mother and friend would come around occasionally to throw food on the ground at his feet and, when he reached for it, they would kick it away from him and laugh.

Now, at age 21, he had begun to treat his girlfriend like his mother had treated him. His mother had reported him, and she was committing him for psychiatric care. In his confused and pent-up rage, he vowed to kill them all.

Not all stories are this extreme, of course. However, some dark and dreadful time bombs tick in distanced and disillusioned young hearts which roll down freeways in fancy automobiles.

Out of sight. Out of touch. Out of line. This left David completely out of control. When his daughter, Tamar, was raped by her brother, David was merely grieved. When Absalom's hands shed Amnon's blood, David was angry. Grieved and angry! But he did nothing! What is a father to do when paralyzed by guilt? How do you punish your sons for copying pages from your own book?

Not Out of Time

Although David was out of control, he was not out of time. True, some of David's sons were dead, but *he* had more time so he zeroed in on Solomon. David was not beyond the circle of God's love. Solomon at this time was not a junior high preteen. He was a man with a family and in line for the throne.

Even so, David had not taken his hands off Solomon's heart—nor had God taken His hands off David.

David charged Solomon:

And you, my son Solomon, acknowledge the God of your father, and serve him with whole-hearted devotion and with a willing mind, for the LORD *searches every heart* and understands every motive behind the thoughts
                    (1 Chronicles 28:9,10).

Too bad David hadn't said these things to Amnon and Absalom!

By this time, though, deep grief had taught him high values. With Solomon, David put some roots straight down through the hard surface of the fast lane.

About the time I hit my mid-forties, our children began to marry and leave us. I dreaded the rapidly approaching day when Chris, our youngest son, would leave home. Everything important to me was slipping into the past. The future seemed to have vaporized.

Then our grandchildren came along. Halle-lujah! Suddenly, everything important in life shifted to the future. I am more eager than ever to teach the ways of God to my sons and daughters and their children. I learned this from David.

Things may not have gone well in your family. Possibly you have been out of sight, out of touch, out of control; but you are not out of time. Maybe it is not too late.

Close this book. Get up and make some phone calls. Circle around you what family you can.

Sit down and say, "I know now that in many ways I have failed you. But could our family have a new start? We can still change the way we live. Let's be family: father, mother, children and grandchildren for the future generations."

One poet said,

An old man, traveling a lone highway,
Came at evening cold and gray
To a chasm vast and deep and wide
That barred his way at eventide.

The old man crossed in the twilight dim;
That turbid stream held no fear for him.
But he turned, when safe on the other side,
And builded a bridge to span the tide.

"Good friend," said a fellow-traveler near,
"You're wasting your time in building here.
You never again will pass this way;
Your journey is over at close of day.
You've crossed your chasm deep and wide.
Why build this bridge at eventide?"

The traveler lifted his old, gray head.
"Good friend, on the way I've come," he said,
"There follows on my path today
A youth who, too, must pass this way.
This stream, which was but naught to me,
To that fair-haired lad may a pitfall be.
He, too, must cross in the twilight dim.
Good friend, I am building this bridge for him."
— Will Allen Dromcoole[6]

Here the familiar poem ends—but it didn't say enough to suit me. Our children grow up in the fast lane where roots are not automatically stimulated and where the challenges to their spiritual development are vastly different from our experiences. So I have taken

the liberty to scratch a few lines of my own to complete
the poem for our times:

> When the youth arrived at the chasm wide,
> He scorned the bridge which spanned the tide.
> "That bridge is obsolete to me,
> I have strength to leap the stream, you see.
>
> "But from my vantage point," he said,
> "I can see that an ocean lies ahead
> Which never presented its challenge to you.
> So how can you help me see it through?"
>
> The old man listened, then nodded his head.
> "You have taught me a lesson today," he said.
> Then traveler and youth worked side by side,
> Ripped planks from the bridge
>   which spanned the tide,
> And from these timbers tried and true,
> They fashioned a vessel to sail the blue.
> Then, driven by winds from the heavens above,
> They challenged the ocean together in love.
>
> (L.A.)

Is it time to take a long, hard look
at your family?
Remember:
They are not beyond the circle
of God's love, and it's never too late
for *some* kind of change.

What do you people mean
by quoting this proverb
about the land of Israel:
"The fathers eat sour grapes,
and the children's teeth
are set on edge"?
—Ezekiel 18:2,3

"The man who has not suffered—
what does he know anyway?"
—Rabbi Abraham Heschel

How children of today (especially adult children), the church, and the crushed parents themselves can help . . .

When a Father's Heart Is Breaking

2 Samuel 18–19

 aving a baby really hurts. Do I hear a mother mumbling, "A lot he knows about it"? Right.

Still, the pain of childbirth, although it lingers only briefly, aptly signals the permanent pain of parenting. *Bearing* a child hurts the mother, but *having* a child for a lifetime will drive both parents through recurring cycles of agony.

171

- A father stares at the ceiling while the seconds drag by. Finally, at 3 A.M., the telephone rings. The desk sergeant is kind, but his words cut deeply. "We are holding your son for bail." Pain.

- Signs appear: Listlessness. Poor grades. Paraphernalia found in her room. Reality must be faced. "Our little dimpled daughter is on drugs." Pain.

- "Daddy, I'm pregnant." Pain.

- "I have AIDS, Mom. Am I going to die?" Pain.

- "We found him dead in his room. Suicide." Pain. Long, slow, unrelenting agony.

Maybe not always this acute, but pain at some level is par for parents.

Our man David knew this. He experienced far more pain from his children than from all his enemies combined. David's tears flowed like a river. David's son raped David's own daughter — a dagger deep in David's heart.

"Amnon, my boy, is dead." Dead by his brother's hand. The king wept, mourning for his son.

"Is the young man safe? Oh, Absalom, my son. Why couldn't I have died rather than you? Oh, Absalom, my son. My son. Oh-h-h." Tears.

David's grief, however, was as much from guilt as bereavement. Being a parent can be, oh, so full of guilt! Maybe you are reading these words today, hurting like David. What do we say when a father's heart is breaking? Maybe nothing of substance. Words usually are little help. Yet we cautiously record a few words here which may rise up through the fog of guilt and confusion to offer hurting parents some comfort.

To the Children

A few words to you who are children. As you read, you may be thinking, *Why address children in this book? Kids don't read this kind of stuff.*

True, little children don't. But sons and daughters do—adults who are still angry with their parents. Absalom was thirty years or more of age when he struck back at his father. Possibly you want your parents to be blamed for your weaknesses and problems, to feel pain as fitting punishment for what they have done to you.

You may also feel that their failures relieve you of responsibility. "After all, what chance have I had? Look at all the blunders my parents made."

Listen up! *You are responsible for what you do.* As your age and independence increase, parental responsibility for you decreases. Dodging responsibility can be as addictive as are alcohol or drugs. Trace Absalom's downward spiral. It is actually a list of choices, each carrying with it increasing adult responsibility.

David was a lousy parent, but he is not culpable for Absalom's crimes. Absalom had "heart" problems. He was self-willed, self-centered and eventually, treacherously wicked—by his own choices. Sure, the mistakes of parents handicap most of us, but why do some children of lousy parents become balanced human beings, while some children of excellent parents run afoul? When does the statute of limitations on bad parenting run out? At 8? 18? 80?

Hold on to your hat. The next suggestion may seem at first to be preposterous.

Why not *forgive your parents?*

Actually, you must. No matter what you feel they have done, if you do not forgive them, you are only choosing to cripple yourself. Some of us love our anger. Rage has become our miserable friend. Besides, we can use our anger as justification for a thousand moral failures.

Let me call on you to forgive. Then *go and specifically tell your parents they are forgiven* and loved, loved deeply. You do love them deeply or they could not have hurt you so deeply to start with.

To the Church

When a father's heart is breaking, the community of believers around him may need help in understanding how to respond.

For example, don't rush in where angels fear to tread. *Speak only into an earned relationship.*

A minister friend of mine once experienced devastating heartbreak as his son plunged into substance abuse. One Sunday morning, during one of the darkest times for the minister and his wife, a parishioner who did not know them well at all accosted my friend in the foyer with, "You've got to stop being so harsh on your son."

My friend struggled to maintain his dissolving composure. He mumbled something like, "Well, please don't stop praying for me."

"Oh, I haven't been praying for you," the would-be counselor/assailant snapped!

Listen! When my heart is breaking over my children, if you have not been praying for me for a long time, please don't advise me.

Prying can be insensitive and damaging as well. Often certain well-meaning but miserable comforters will probe, requiring pained parents to relive their pain over and over. Be a listener, but allow hurting parents to decide how much they want to talk.

Timing is delicate, too. The right moment to speak will best be recognized within the context of a long and meaningful relationship.

Also, *be careful where you brag!* Your good family may almost seem an indictment to the parent whose heart is breaking. It can devastate a parent in pain to look at the smiling photographs of another person's healthy children and hear a litany of their virtues and achievements.

The *quick answer doesn't help,* either. Easy answers to tough problems don't really answer. As I write these words I cringe, remembering some of my recommendations to devastated parents. Once I recall stopping dead in the middle of a monologue about how we had dealt with our kids, realizing how far off base I was. The context for their children didn't remotely resemble ours. Besides, I really don't have the foggiest notion why our children seem well-adjusted and spiritually alive at this point in our lives. Mostly, it has been blind luck and "amazing grace." The development of human personality is a mystery too profound to be understood, let alone to be packaged and franchised.

Dr. Paul Faulkner says, "When my child acts up, *don't criticize me.* Help me." After all, criticism often falls wide of the mark anyway.

Good Kids/Bad Kids

Our married son, looking back on his high school years, noted an interesting phenomenon. Some kids in his school were popular, Mister-Big-Man-on-Campus types. They avoided the riffraff kids, but often only for political reasons. Some of these managed to maintain the Mister-Clean image, while at the same time doing the same things the riffraff did: drinking, having sex, cheating, even doing some drugs, and using friends as means to their own ends.

Some of the other kids on campus, the "other group," did run with the wrong crowd, and did some acting out with them, yet they were people-sensitive and they experienced genuine caring relationships.

In later years, some of those in the second group got their behavior together and went right on serving people. Many of those in the first group maintained their facades, kept their images intact, stopped some of their bad habits, but went right on using people. Yet today group *A* is viewed as "good kids" and group *B* as "bad kids."

Our standards for good kids may also be very different from God's standards. For example, we often whisper behind the hand about Susie's premarital pregnancy, while Johnny habitually sasses his parents, and we see that as no big deal. However, the law of God dealt redemptively with Susie, making provision for marriage, but the same law said kids who sassed their parents should be stoned to death! We had best criticize cautiously.

Rather than advice and criticism, parents in pain *need someone who will simply listen.* When my father's heart (my heart as a father) is breaking, I need to know I am loved by people who hurt with me and who affirm my worth as a person no matter how incorrigible my children may seem. Just be there.

To the Crushed Parents

Dare I attempt a word directly to crushed and brokenhearted parents? For some of your kids, the jury is still out. Adolescence is a stormy and unpredictable time. A child need not be typecast on the basis of one chaotic period in his or her life.

David, a youth minister friend of mine, went recently to lead a youth rally at the Christian high school I once attended. A mother of two rebellious adolescents tearfully approached David, brokenhearted over her children. In an attempt to comfort her, he reminded her that the script had not all been written yet, and that, with patience and time, rebellious adolescents often blossom into happy, healthy adults.

The lady dabbed at her tears, grinned knowingly, and said, "That is what our principal told me. He said a few years back there was a kid so incorrigible that everyone had given up on him; they should have kicked him out of school — but they didn't. His name was Lynn Anderson." Parents and others who waited patiently while the "jury was still out" loom majestically important to me now.

In Proverbs 22:6, Solomon said, "When he is old, he will not depart" (literally, "when he has a beard"). Often the seeds of faith and value which were planted in the heart of a child will germinate and flourish in adult years.

However, for many parents the jury already has brought in the verdict: The damage is irreparable. Relationships are too far gone. Faith is destroyed. Substance abuse. Mental illness. Crime. Prison. AIDS. Maybe even suicide. What is there for a father whose heart is permanently broken?

One thing is sure. That father need not beat himself over the head with a superficial and damaging view of that famous "parent's proverb" mentioned above: "Train up a child in the way he should go, and when he is old he will not depart from it." Abuse of this passage keeps the red guilt-light flashing. "My child did depart; therefore, I must be to blame."

A proverb, by literary definition, is not a promise. Nor a rule. Nor a judgment. Proverbs are "collections of wise and ancient sayings which are generally true" — but not always. Why do some parents have three beautifully adjusted children, and another who is a complete disaster? Did they perfectly train up three and totally fail on the fourth?

Other Influences

While we are clubbing people with proverbs, why not swing some which speak to the child's accountability for his own choices? "A wise son heeds his father's instruction, but a mocker does not listen to rebuke" (Proverbs 13:1). This one makes the child culpable! Who *is* to blame here, Solomon?

When a father's heart is breaking, he need not add the overwhelming weight of guilt to his already unbearable burden of grief. Other forces besides parents are at work in the lives of our children. The mothers of David's children influenced their lives, too. His kids played for hours in streets with all kinds of outside influences around them. Absalom spent three crucial years in Geshur, where his grandfather likely helped him plot the attempted overthrow of David. Our children, too, spend six to eight hours per day in environments other than our homes. Celebrity role models shape our children's self-awareness: athletes, rock musicians, actors. Music and movies also affect kids. So do schoolteachers. A recent survey reveals that children watch television an average of five hours a day, and by graduation a high school student has viewed 22,000 hours of television.[1] Possibly the most irresistible influence of all is peer pressure.

Children are shaped by their whole environment. The voice of the parent is only one voice among the crowd.

Besides, our children are not robots who can be programmed, even if we nailed every parenting technique perfectly. If poor Absalom was simply the victim of David's lousy parenting, then Absalom is not to blame. But what of David's failures? Are they not his father Jesse's fault? Where then did Jesse get his warts? How many generations do we go back? Did someone say "All the way to Adam"? True. The first parents fouled up even while they were still in Eden.

Can we go one step further? If parents are the only factor, then God was a parental failure. Look at Adam. Look at the lot of us. No. Each of us answers for

his own sins. The Bible makes that clear through Ezekiel, the prophet:

> What do you people mean by quoting this
> proverb . . . "The fathers eat sour grapes, and
> the children's teeth are set on edge"?
> (Ezekiel 18:1,2).

> The soul who sins is the one who will die
> (verse 4*b*).

> Suppose there is a righteous man
> who does what is just and right . . .
> He will surely live,
>   declares the Sovereign LORD (verses 5,9).

> Suppose he has a violent son, who sheds blood
> or does any of these other things (though the
> father has done none of them) . . . Will such a
> man live? He will not! . . . He will surely be put
> to death and his blood will be on his own head
> (verses 10,11,13).

Forgiving Ourselves

Paul the apostle declares that when we stand
before the judgment, "each one [will] receive what is
due him for the things [individually] done while in the
body" (2 Corinthians 5:10).

No, dear crushed parent, the ancient proverb
does not hold you fully responsible for the way your
child will go. You need not compound your grief with
guilt.

Sure, there is some guilt. We parents are all
guilty in a thousand ways, many of which we will never
be aware. We can only turn to God's grace—to His
mercies, which never come to an end. When a father's
heart is breaking, he needs to accept God's forgiveness.

Brokenhearted parents need to forgive them-selves. Of course we are guilty — but Jesus took our load. We need not make guilt a miserable and destructive old "friend."

Why not verbalize specifically what we know we have done wrong? Write it down. Tell God and at least one other person exactly what you need to forgive yourself for. "Confess your sins to each other . . . so that you may be healed" (James 5:16).

Asking Forgiveness From Our Child

Where this is still possible, our specific fail-ures should be confessed to our child, even our adult child, and his or her forgiveness asked. I find myself these days in the confessing stage of parenthood. All our children are gone from home. Adults. Still, I frequently surface a pain which I must confess to them and for which I must ask their forgiveness. In fact, just this past week I made one of those calls.

Our oldest son had found early high school a difficult time. He was small for his age, plus we had moved and he was in a new school away from childhood friends in the tenth grade. He lacked self-confidence then, but one of the things he loved and did well was to build things with his hands. He and I planned a pen for our bird dog. Jon loved the building project, completing a good share of it while I was away one week. When I returned, he proudly led me out to see his work. Then I began my critique. "That's not how we planned the foundation. That gate will never hang straight."

Jon's head sank lower and lower, as he pre-tended to be working on some materials at his feet. When he raised his face, his lips were quivering, and tears filled his hurt eyes. "But, Dad. It's just the first one I ever built, you know."

Not till long afterward did I fully realize what I had done to Jon that day. So I called him last week in Colorado — called my son, who is now a fine man — and confessed that sin to him. Confessed and begged his forgiveness. Likely I'll be periodically making this sort of call to one or the other of my children as long as I live. I've got to. Besides deepening our relationship, it helps me to forgive myself.

Giving Forgiveness

Maybe you need to forgive your mate. Yes, parents sometimes blame each other for children gone wrong. Often we swallow the accusations, smoldering with anger at our mate, choking back an old and bitter rage. John White, in his book, *Parents in Pain*, says that "problem children put horrendous strain on marriages."[2] The strain is often there, even when neither party is able to acknowledge it or put a finger on it.

Of course, no one parent makes all the mistakes. In fact, if I see my wife as always the culprit, I may be revealing a trait in my nature that is indeed the very point at which I failed with the children. Still, even if I had a report from a family therapist and a sworn statement from "Good Housekeeping," signed by ten angels, stating the total guilt of my mate, I have no choice on what I must do: I must forgive my mate — today! I must, or I will not find healing and will never have the heart to go on.

When a father's heart is breaking, he may also need to forgive his child. Often parents don't forgive. A grown woman tells how, years before when she was a teenager, she had become pregnant and then had an abortion. The guilt gnawed at her dreadfully, and she finally poured out the whole sad story to her mother. Her mother flew into a rage and retreated to her room, closing the door. The mother stayed in the room for days. When she finally emerged, she refused to discuss the matter again. Though the daughter is now an adult with her own family, the relationship between her and her mother has never been healed.

One adult, after years of alcohol abuse, arrests, and expensive court costs, is finally a recovered and healthy human being. Even so, his aging parents regularly remind him, "You are the reason we have no retirement left." They need to forgive him. This is the only way to a whole relationship with God.

After all, our heavenly Father is the ultimate example of the forgiving parent. "God demonstrates his own love for us in this: While we were still sinners, Christ died for us" (Romans 5:8). God moves out along the roadways of life, pursuing and forgiving His lost children who have hurt Him so. When the Father is not searching the roads, He is preparing forgiveness parties for prodigals!

Why not have a family forgiveness party, with confessions, tears, and specific forgiveness all around? God does.

David sat mourning alone. His armies crept back into town, as if they had been defeated. Morale was slipping; chaos and mutiny threatened. But Joab said, "David, you are still valuable as a person. We need you. Your army needs you. Israel needs you. Get on with your life, David. If your grief continues to paralyze you, greater disaster will befall you" (see 2 Samuel 19:1-8).

David found the heart to go on. He pulled himself together, again put on his crown and royal robes, and resumed his place as king. Strangely, David's suffering only made him a better king and a richer resource for the ages. As Greek tragedy says:

> Day by day, bit by bit, pain drips upon the heart as against our will and even in our own despite comes wisdom from the awful grace of the gods.
>
> —Aeschylus

A father who carries his wounds of guilt and whose children continue to inflict fresh pain on him will always walk with a limp—but other people need him and will respect him. Although his child may be dead—gone forever—a father may have more to offer than ever before. Once he has come to terms with his pain, he will be capable of great comfort to others.

> Praise be to the . . . God of all comfort, who comforts us in all our troubles, so that we can comfort those in any trouble with the comfort we ourselves have received from God
>
> (2 Corinthians 1:3,4).

If you need help in forgiving,
or in accepting forgiveness,
Remember:
God's grace and mercy
never come to an end.

Then David's men swore to him, saying,
"Never again will you go out with us to battle,
so that the lamp of Israel
will not be extinguished."
—*2 Samuel 21:17b*

TWELVE

David exemplifies how to adapt
to a new phase of our lives . . .

Aging With Class

1 Samuel 21

 QUESTION: Who was Fred Biletnikoff? ANSWER: Wide receiver for the Oakland Raiders.

QUESTION: Who was Christopher Columbus? ANSWER: The man who discovered America.

If these are your answers, you are wrong on both counts. A wide receiver is not who Fred was, but something he did. Christopher Columbus discovered America, but who was the person?

There is a vast difference between what we do and who we are. What I do is what you see in a couple

187

of hours as you read this book. Who I am my wife Carolyn has to live with every day.

You have heard vocation confused with personhood a thousand times. "Let me introduce George Smith, president of International Properties." Then retirement day comes. George gets a gold watch, a forty-year pin, and a round of applause. Now, who is he? Nobody, that's who.

When athletes, executives, surgeons, entertainers or farmers can no longer do what they do, they are benched, where at best they may become benign and bored or at worst they become bitter. Twin tragedies result: Aging persons get dehumanized and society loses valuable resources. The younger desperately need those older.

One day our friend King David was given his gold watch and thirty-year pin and sent home from the action, too. The whole thing came about, as it often does, without David's choosing, and as a humiliating surprise.

David, the Warrior

At the time, David sat firmly on the throne. Wealth was accumulating. Power was growing. His empire was expanding. Another battle broke out on the Philistine front, and the old warrior buckled on his sword and, as usual, headed for the action. But by this time David was more than 60 years of age. He had run out of gas. The old stamina stalled and the magnificent reflexes failed.

Spotting David in his exhausted state, an opportunistic cousin of Goliath seized the moment. The

Philistine would have killed David had not Abishai come to the old man's rescue. How much humiliation can a proud warrior handle in one day?

"Thanks, Abishai. I blew that one. Could have taken him easily, but the worn cleats on these old war boots . . . I slipped, Abishai. Abishai?"

How could it be? Where is David the warrior? Is this David, son of Jesse, who felled Goliath? Is this the man who brought two hundred Philistine foreskins in a sack and slammed them down on Saul's desk, double dowry for the king's daughter, while the women sang, "Saul has slain his thousands, and David his tens of thousands" (1 Samuel 18:7)?

In his prime David had been no ordinary fighting man. He terrorized the countryside. Around him were six hundred crack troops, led by thirty mighty men, each with the strength of a hundred men. All had been afraid of David. Is this David tired? Does this warrior need help in a fight with just one ordinary Philistine?

I feel an awkward silence fall. As David's officers quietly encircle him, gathering the courage for a long overdue confrontation, who spoke first? Abishai? Joab?

"My Lord, my King. We . . . we're all your friends, so aside with the formality. David, the time has come for you to hang up your sword. Go home. Close the book. This chapter of yours is finished. We all swear to you, David; you need to go home. Now. For your own good. And for Israel."

The eyes of his officers, first avoiding David's face, were now leveled directly at him. This circle of men loved him, but somehow their combined fixed gazes, for the first time in his life, were intimidating.

"But I just slipped. Go home? Ah, yes, I guess. Sooner or later. Now?"

More silence. The leveled eyes of David's lifetime friends sealed the question. How does an old warrior feel at such a time? He hesitated, and then slowly slid his rusty sword into its sheath for the last time. In resignation, he exhaled a long breath. He stumbled toward the chariot and stiffly dragged himself up. Wheels rumbled on rocks. David's lone figure sat slouch-shouldered as the chariot bore him over the horizon toward Jerusalem, sent home from his last battle, defeated.

Gold watch. Forty-year pin. Golf clubs. David, go home — and stay there!

A glance in the mirror confirmed their advice. No young redheaded warrior stared back from David's looking glass, but an aging man with silver locks and furrowed cheeks. Where great plates of muscle once spanned David's chest, now ribs showed through and loose flab sagged at his middle. The warrior was gone!

David, the Lamp

But wait! Did our old soldier go home to sulk away his later years? Not our David. He was already dreaming bigger dreams than ever. He loved more deeply, enriching his relationships. Most important, David, in his sunset years, grew increasingly alive to God. He prepared for the temple, buying land, drawing plans, and equipping personnel. He trained musicians and arranged psalms toward the time when praises of Yahweh would ring day and night in the temple courts.

Some of David's finest poetry flowed from his pen during his golden post-warrior days. His wisdom deepened. Perspective enriched his insights. He would write:

> The righteous will flourish like a palm tree . . .
> They will still bear fruit in old age,
>   they will stay fresh and green . . .

Why did this old warrior not "retire" and vegetate after the "useful years of his career" were over? What made David different from most millions? The answer lies in the last half of a sentence we interrupted a couple of pages ago. True, David's men did swear to him saying, "Never again will you go out with us to battle," but that was only part of what they said. The last half of the sentence explains:

> . . . so that the lamp of Israel will not be
> extinguished (Psalm 92:12-14).

David was not sent home because his usefulness was over. Rather David's men sent him home because of his usefulness. He was too valuable to Israel to be risked in battle. Be careful not to miss this. David saw his own identity clearly, so he did not pine away in oblivion. He did not define himself as "warrior." Soldiering was something he did for a certain period of his life, but not who he was. Rather, David saw his real identity as "Lamp of Israel." That's who he was.

He was a man after God's own heart, who not only gave light to Israel in the flesh in the long ago, but he also became a "lamp" for all men, everywhere, for all time. When hearts ache for comfort and eyes long for sight, to what pages have God's people for centuries turned to read? Have they flipped over to the battle legends of the "warrior"? No. They have read and reflected upon the poems and songs radiating from the "Lamp of Israel." They still do.

To their great credit, David's men saw that the true heart of the kingdom was a spiritual heart. They valued David's person over his prowess, his spiritual resources over his physical energy. They clearly understood that the hope of Israel lay with the spiritual lamp at its heart, not with the sword swingers at its frontiers. As a result, David aged with class and the kingdom was kept on course.

In Our Day

In twentieth-century Western culture, our value system is turned bottom side up.

We are the informational society. Progress is productivity. Productivity requires power, so we place our priority on youth, energy, looks and ambition—a total reversal from David and his men. This dehumanizes the aging. Some aging men cling desperately to youthful positions, finally losing their grip and their dignity. Others retire meekly to oblivion.

What is worse, the church becomes involved. A community of faith taken captive by culture is a compounded tragedy. Our religious adjectives betray us. Dynamic. Aggressive. Energetic. Active. Successful. These describe ministers and churches.

This means, of course, that churches, too, place priority on youth. We want warriors, not lamps.

When youthful vigor declines, we cast old lamps aside, and then these tragedies result:

First, the organic body of Christ often becomes distorted until it resembles a corporation.

Second, the elderly are left to sit and wait — for nothing.

Third, and most tragic of all, the community of believers attempts to operate on the "arm of flesh," ignoring its richest resources.

Yet from God's perspective, only age can generate the real valuables. Youthful energy produces, all right, but it produces superficial things. We must rediscover the difference between a lamp and a warrior. The church is not a corporation geared to productivity, creating careers and consuming youthful energy. Rather, the church is a family which grows through enriched relationships. The church is a body with eyes, heart and spirit. The church does not so much need its crank turned as it needs its darkness illuminated by the lamps of Israel.

Age can be loaded with spiritual resources. Time supplies perspective. David hints toward this: "I was young and now I am old" (Psalm 37:25). Years on the road gather experience, as blind alleys are checked out, temptations overcome, and skills learned.

With age, serious believers become our valuable mentors. Young believers, tempted to defect, can look up and see, ahead of them on the way, a gray head which has felt infinitely more pain, discouragement and temptation than have the young, but is still believing, still traveling toward God.

Those of advanced years supply the rich memories which are the roots of dreams. Of course.

> Is not wisdom found among the aged? Does not
> long life bring understanding? (Job 12:12)

Without the lamps of Israel at the heart of the kingdom, the warriors on the frontiers may continue to swing their swords awhile, but to diminishing avail.

Prizing Spiritual Depth

The straight message for those people who are younger is this: Prize spiritual depth over high energy.

Seek out the older folks who sparkle, and beat a path to their door. Ask them many questions about the mysteries of life. Listen carefully, not just politely.

The young may also want to revamp the very structures of the church, and of society, for that matter. Create forms which tap the resources of age rather than sideline them. One retired physician who was also an elder in our church, resigned from being an elder, he said, so that he could "do more shepherding." How ludicrous! This man, and many other spiritual giants, retire from church leadership as age advances because they don't have the energy to attend a hundred meetings a year. What has that to do with anything?

Ed and Kathryn, a retired couple in our church, have been spending forty hours per week, for more than ten years, running off cassette tapes of messages and classes, labeling and mailing them to the far-flung corners of the globe. They dread the rapidly approaching day when "we will no longer have the energy to do this, and we will be so useless."

Why should they not gladly lay down the sword in order to make their lamps available to the younger ones? Enormous value could be gained by couples like these spending those forty hours a week simply giving counsel, answering questions, offering encouragement, as younger strugglers emerge from the ring of darkness just beyond the lamp's pool of warm light.

I dream of a special kind of pleasant park under an atrium, featuring alcoves and chairs and tables. Old and young meet here. At all hours of the day older people are available to the younger who come streaming in, exuding energy but needing spiritual resources. As they bask in the light of the aged, the young discuss work, marriage, children. They find wisdom regarding heartache, money, sex. They come asking for resources to confront temptation, loneliness, suffering. The young want to hear the seasoned believers talk about death, heaven, doubt. Something like this could turn our culture right side up again.

Your Real Worth

The straight message to the older ones is this: Trust what the Word says about your value to those of us who are younger. We need the energy of your spirits in our deep places where the physical energy of our youth is inadequate. Your advanced years are too valuable to waste, my friends. Don't cling to youth or mourn lost energy. Go home from the wars and be something far more important than a warrior. Be a lamp in Israel.

One of our sons-in-law has a dream. His goal is to be financially independent by age 40 so he can spend the rest of his life, self-supported, in full-time ministry. If at 40 why not at 65? Why not retire to full-time, self-supporting ministry? The fact is, you have no right to withhold your spiritual resources from the family of God. We need you. We feel better when you are near.

Ronald Reagan turned 70 just seventeen days after entering the office of President of the United States. Prior to Reagan, the oldest president to be elected was Henry Harrison in 1840. He was 68. Unfortunately, President Harrison caught cold on Inauguration Day and, due to his exhausted condition from the campaign, never recovered. He died one month later. Since then we as a nation have tended to shy away from older men and have chosen younger men to be our leaders.

But Ronald Reagan has put the lie to all that. Actually, he merely underscored the long testimony of the centuries. Abraham left Ur at 70 years of age. Aaron was 83 when he and his 80-year-old brother, Moses, left Egypt. Toscanini was 87 and still directing a symphony orchestra. Edison was busy in his lab at 83. Benjamin Franklin governed Pennsylvania at 79. Winston Churchill led Great Britain at 76. Albert Schweitzer was still practicing missionary medicine at 90. Jomo Kenyata made Kenya the outstanding African nation when he was president at 80.

Laura Ingalls Wilder, wrote most of the stories which became TV's *Little House on the Prairie* during her 70- to 90-age years. Cecil B. deMille produced the movie *Ten Commandments* at age 75. Anna Mary Moses decided at 76 that she was bored with knitting, and she took up painting. After that time "Grandma Moses" produced more than a thousand paintings. Michelangelo created St. Peter's Basilica in Rome after he was 70. Some of George Burns' best years are the other side of 80.

While some of these accomplishments did demand enormous physical energy, surely the greater treasures of age are spiritual resources which soar in the latest years of life, after energy dissipates.

The Greater Value

Remember, David was not sent home from the battlefield because his usefulness was over, but because his nature as Man of God and Lamp of Israel was far more important and permanent than his role as warrior.

In an ancient Taoist legend, a carpenter and his apprentice looked at a huge oak which was very old and very gnarled.

The carpenter said to his apprentice, "Do you know why this tree is so big and so old?"

The apprentice answered, "No. Why?"

The carpenter answered, "Because it is useless. If it were useful, it would have been cut down, sawed up and used for beds and tables and chairs. But because it is useless, it has been allowed to grow. And that is why it is now so great that you can rest in its shadow."[1]

Trees are most useful and beautiful as trees, not as furniture.

My friend and brother Earl Kiser is 97 years old, can no longer be our church custodian, and lives in a rest home. He has read the Word and walked and talked with God virtually every day of his literate life.

I am glad he wasn't sawed and cut into benches, because
I need to sit in his shade. He can barely shuffle along,
pushing that old walker, but I feel better when he is in
the room. I need him. The fact that he no longer has the
energy to clean our church building doesn't mean he
has lost his value to our church family.

To Earl Kiser and to all those who have lived
quite a long time, longer than some of the rest of us: We
need you—desperately.

We need to sit in your shade.

We need you to be our lamps.

Are you approaching what others might call
your "sunset years"?
Remember:
God has a distinct purpose for you,
no matter what your age,
and He will provide your needs
to meet that purpose.

*If you forgive men
when they sin against you,
your heavenly Father will also forgive you.
But if you do not forgive men their sins,
your Father will not forgive your sins.*
—*Matthew 6:14,15*

THIRTEEN

The drama of David's struggle with grudges
reminds us that we all are complex creatures . . .

Trying to Forgive

2 Samuel 19

ot long ago I sat in a car with a man from Oregon and listened as he poured out an agonizing story of hurt. The wife of his son had become entangled in a wild and public affair with another man. Tongues wagged through the whole community. The children heard. The son was so crushed he could scarcely function.

The family is back together now. Repentance. Confessions. Apologies. Counseling and therapy have repair well under way. The marriage is growing again. But the father looked at me and said, "How do I get rid of the hatred? I carry this knife in my pocket," he said, flicking open a wicked-looking blade, "for him—for that guy who tried to steal my son's wife."

Levels of Forgiveness

We all find forgiveness exceedingly difficult. Sometimes forgiveness comes so hard that we can release our grudges only one level at a time. This means forgiveness is often granted only at superficial levels. These are *qualified* forgivenesses. A key word is *if*. "I'll forgive you, *if* you show proper remorse." "*If* you do what I think you ought to do to clean up your mess, I'll forgive you."

Another key word is *when*. "I'll forgive you *when* I am able. You've got to give me some time to work through this." What we may really mean is, "I want to let you stew in your own juice awhile first."

A second level is *partial* forgiveness. The key word here is *but*. "I'll forgive you, *but* . . . please get out of my life." "I forgave him, *but* you surely don't expect me to treat him the same again."

Let me challenge you to sit down and make a list of people you find difficult to forgive. I have to nearly every day. Either in your mind, or on a piece of paper, make your list. Maybe the list will include a coach who didn't play you. You knew you had earned that spot, but he left you on the bench game after game and it still burns in your gut. Maybe you'll list a boss who always blamed someone else's mistakes on you, so that you marginally held on to your job while the raises and promotions went to the other guy. Ten years have passed, but you have never really been able to forget. Or years ago someone started a rumor about you which has been dogging your steps ever since. Or a mate put you down. Or a child broke your heart. Or a parent broke your spirit.

Whatever it is, put it on the list. Are you thinking this asks too much? Now wait—before you scrub the idea, let's go to the Bible.

The testimony of David's experience is that you will never have real freedom until you deal with the forgiveness problem. A remembered *offense* broods its way into a *resentment,* which often grows into a *grudge.* A grudge easily festers into *hatred,* and hatred can lead to *revenge.*

Another Drama

An ancient drama unfolds in three colorful scenes, with three major characters: a spiteful little bully by the name of Shimei; a king, David; and his military officer Abishai.

The first scene opens as *David* flees from Jerusalem upon the humiliating and terrifying news that Absalom's uprising is at the gates of the city. With his royal dignity in the dust, David ran. And as David and his friends fled through the countryside, their road led them past the walls of Bahurim. At David's approach, enter the second character: *Shimei,* a relative of Saul. Shimei . . .

> cursed as he came out. He pelted David and all
> the king's officials with stones . . . As he cursed,
> Shimei said, "Get out, get out, you man of
> blood, you scoundrel! The LORD has repaid you
> for all the blood you shed in the household of
> Saul . . . The LORD has handed the kingdom
> over to your son, Absalom (2 Samuel 16:5-8).

Shimei carried two lies on his tongue: First, David had not been slaughtering the household of Saul; and second, the Lord did not give Jerusalem to Absalom—Absalom had stolen the throne away from David. One could scarcely fault David for disliking Shimei. Every life will have its occasional Shimei.

Enter our third character, *Abishai*, David's close bodyguard since the days in the desert when David was running from Saul. Abishai held a fierce loyalty with a low flash point.

> Then Abishai . . . said to the king, "Why should this dead dog curse my lord the king? Let me go over and cut off his head" (verse 9).

Violence had always been Abishai's style of conflict resolution: Swing your sword and lop off your problem. For every Shimei who appears in life, a corresponding Abishai will be waiting to feed bitterness and even volunteer to implement revenge.

Now back to character one: David. Ah, David. He said to Abishai and all his officials, "Leave him alone; let him curse, for the LORD has told him to" (verse 11).

Wow! When someone is being unfair to you, have you ever thought, *Maybe* the *Lord* wants him to do this? Surely David was not merely thick-skinned; rather, he was bighearted. He had the authority and the manpower to smear Shimei across the landscape—but David was too big to do it.

Some time back I heard Charles Swindoll relate a legend concerning John D. Rockefeller. It seems that one of the top executives in Rockefeller's company made a two-million-dollar mistake—on one Friday. By

Monday everyone was tiptoeing around the office avoiding the closed oak door behind which they were sure an infuriated Rockefeller lurked, ready to pounce on the first victim to get his attention.

Finally, one of the executives had no choice; a matter required personal conversation with John D. himself. The man tapped gently on the door, and a friendly voice called, "Come in."

When the oak door opened, the nervous executive saw Rockefeller sitting at his desk, calmly working some figures. The intruder mustered the courage to ask, "You heard there was a costly mistake, didn't you?"

"Yes," Rockefeller said, "I heard that. In fact, I've been sitting here figuring it up. Over the last few years that man has made for this company many times the money he lost. I think a guy like him ought to be forgiven this one, don't you?"

What a magnanimous gesture! A two-million-dollar forgiveness. How much like the heart of David. He could have destroyed Shimei, but instead he respected God's hand in the situation and would not strike back.

> So David and his men continued along the road
> while Shimei was going along the hillside op-
> posite him, cursing as he went and throwing
> stones at him and showering him with dirt"
>   (2 Samuel 16:13).

So ends scene one: A compelling and tidy story of amazing forgiveness. Or is it?

Scene Two

"And now, page two," as Paul Harvey would say.

Between scenes one and two, Absalom's army has been defeated and Absalom has been slaughtered. David has plummeted into mourning until Joab snaps him out of his grief and back to acting like a king. Then David sets out toward Jerusalem to reclaim his throne. The rising spirits of David's friends transform the journey into a recoronation party, as "the men of Judah" come out to "meet the king and bring him across the Jordan" (2 Samuel 19:15).

Re-enter Shimei, the bully from Bahurim. Notice this string of panicky verbs: "He hurried down . . . to meet King David . . . they rushed to the Jordan . . . they crossed at the ford . . . Shimei fell prostrate before the king," and he begs for forgiveness (2 Samuel 19:14-20).

Shimei is in a desperate hurry to make things right. He has milked David's vulnerability for all he can, but fortunes shift with lightning speed. Now people swarm out of the villages and fall in behind David, triumphantly bringing him back to Jerusalem. Shimei, who now sees the whole countryside bristling with David's power, totally changes his tune. His terror drags him to a burbling and pathetic apology: "I have sinned," he says—the very words which once had come from David's own mouth.

Re-enter Abishai. Do you hear a sword sliding forcefully from its sheath? Abishai's explosive temper erupts again: "Shouldn't Shimei be put to death for this? He cursed the LORD's anointed" (verse 21). Come on, David, he kicked you when you were down. Now you've got 'im where you want 'im.

I readily identify with Abishai. Under these circumstances my sword would also spring to my hand. But David does not allow Abishai to rain on his parade. "This day you have become my adversaries! Should anyone be put to death in Israel today?" (verse 22).

"Abishai, are you trying to spoil my recoronation party? What would folks think if the king walked back into town swatting mere flies along the way?"

David carefully chooses his words: "So the king said to Shimei, 'You shall not die.' And the king promised him on oath" (verse 23). He speaks the exact words God's prophet Nathan had spoken when David had himself said, "I have sinned." Forgiveness usually flows most freely from a person who has received the most forgiveness. What else could David say?

Scene Three

What a compelling story! Scene one. Scene two. Three characters. Magnanimous gesture by David. Forgiveness. And David fades off into the sunset, while the credits roll up. Or so it would seem. But we have not yet reached scene three! Again, as Paul Harvey would say, "This is the *rest* of the story."

The finale opens in the royal chambers as the aged King David lies on his deathbed. In these final hours he calls his son to his bedside. David's affections and dreams are wrapped up in Solomon.

> When the time drew near for David to die, he gave a charge to Solomon his son. "I am about to go the way of all the earth," he said. "So be

strong, show yourself a man, and observe what the LORD your God requires" (1 Kings 2:1-3).

Fine advice for a father to pass on to his son. "Serve God, Son. Be a good man." However, this isn't all David said. "Oh, by the way. Your poor old daddy has a couple of other minor requests from here on his deathbed. Make sure you repay Joab for the bad things he did to friends of mine." Yes . . .

> Remember . . . Shimei son of Gera, the Benjamite from Bahurim, who called down bitter curses on me the day I went to Mahanaim . . . do not consider him innocent (1 Kings 2:8,9).

Oh, David, why? You had me going there for a while. I mean, two colorful stories about your great forgiving heart, and now this? In 1 Kings, these are David's last recorded words: "You will know what to do to him. Bring his gray head down to the grave in blood" (verse 9).

As David knew, Solomon understood how to exterminate Shimei with finesse. For some time after David's death Solomon did nothing. Three years went by. Then one day the king said to Shimei:

> "You know in your heart all the wrong you did to my father David. Now the LORD will repay you . . . " Then the king gave the order to Benaiah . . . and he went out and struck Shimei down and killed him (1 Kings 2:44-46).

David? David!

Complex Creatures

David had apparently tried with all of his *heart* to forgive Shimei and, from external evidence, appeared to have accomplished that forgiveness. Possibly even David himself thought the resentment was all cleaned out of his heart. The fact is, David took a grudge with him to the grave.

That grudge of David's reminds us that human beings are incredibly complex creatures. Few, if any of us will ever be able to comprehend all that goes on in our own hearts. Just about the time we have ourselves convinced we have finally forgiven the one who has wronged us, that person pops up in surprise circumstances and all the collected hurts rush back in. Your mate may say something to you which sounds almost innocent. Almost. And a whole world of resentment will come down on his or her head. Possibly we think we have forgiven a brother or sister, but when push comes to shove, we are not comfortable in the same room with that person.

Yet looming above David's bitterness is the overwhelming grace and patience of God. I draw comfort from the fact that God kept accepting David in spite of the convoluted forces wrestling in David's soul.

This, of course, is not meant as encouragement to carry grudges to the grave but to bring them to the cross. We enjoy an enormous advantage over David. The law, well known to David, required forgiveness, but Jesus, unknown to David, showed us *how* to forgive. "The straight of it," taught Jesus, "is that you should love your enemies."

But how, Jesus?

Doing Forgiveness

"Pray for those who misuse you. Return good for the evil that's done to you. You must *do* forgiveness." We *do* our way into better feelings. We do not feel our way into better doing. If we wait until all that bitterness is swept out of the corners of our feelings before we do right by someone who has hurt us, we might just as well give up. The bad feelings may never completely go away. But if we begin now dealing with that person, as if he had been totally forgiven and as if all the bad feelings were gone, giving him full personhood and affirmation, somehow the bitterness eventually dissipates. Jesus didn't just *tell* us how to forgive, He *showed* us how on the cross.

Corrie Ten Boom relates her difficult struggle between resentment and forgiveness. As two young Dutch Christians, Corrie and her sister were incarcerated in Nazi war camps during World War II. They were subjected to unspeakable abuse. One guard was especially cruel. He was the man who watched the doorway to the women's showers. More than once this man brutalized both Corrie and her sister.

After the war Corrie tried to drive those memories from her heart, to forgive, and to leave those memories behind. One day as she was traveling through Europe on a postwar speaking tour and was surrounded by a crowd of people, a voice in the crowd called out a number. She froze, instantly recognizing the voice of the shower-room guard.

Then, wheeling toward the voice, she found herself looking directly into the face which had so often been contorted with cruelty—but something was different. The man said, "Corrie Ten Boom, I have been looking all over Europe for you. Since those dark days I have found Jesus. God has forgiven me. Now I am trying to find every person from the camp and beg his forgiveness. Corrie, I have sinned so deeply against you. Could you forgive me?"

All those scenes from the prison sprang to life again. She looked down. She just could not feel forgiving. The man took her by the arm and begged again, "Would you forgive me?" Corrie glanced up into that face, then looked down again, her mind flooded with horrible pictures and her emotions with deep hurt. A third time. "Would you forgive me? Please forgive me."

Great Grace

Corrie said, "I looked down. And it seemed in my mind's eye that I saw a fresh vision of the cross. I saw my Lord hanging there. I saw Him looking into my eyes and He was saying, 'Father, forgive them, because they do not know what they are doing.' And somehow, God gave me the grace to forgive."

When David lay on his death bed, he didn't know the cross. But we know. We know.

At this point our hearts may be touched and our hopes awakened. However, we may still have a formless morass of feelings, looking for a handle. We may have tried it all before. We may have tried silence, indifference, subtle manipulation, or even open revenge. We don't have to live that way forever. Forgiveness is not easy, but it is possible with and through the cross of Jesus Christ.

Say forgiveness out loud. Where is your list? Dig up the list you made at the beginning of this chapter. Find the people you need to forgive and tell them they are forgiven. Tell God you forgive them. Make a specific list of things you need to forgive; dredge them up and get rid of them. When you have finished praying over your list, burn it! Get rid of it forever. Forgive. Forgiveness begins with a decision of the will.

In a little town in Kentucky lives a couple named Frank and Elizabeth Morris. They are members of the Little River Church, where Frank is the song leader. For more than two years Frank and Elizabeth dedicated their lives to punishing the drunken driver Tommy Pigage, "who killed our only child."

Driven by hatred, they monitored his every court appearance. They followed him to the county jail to make sure he was serving his weekend sentences. They watched his apartment, hoping to catch him violating probation. "We wanted him in prison," Mrs. Morris confessed. "No, we wanted him dead!"

They were expecting swift justice but the grand jury handed them their first disappointment, reducing the murder charge to second-degree manslaughter.

Finally, Circuit Judge Edwin White ordered Tommy Pigage to spend every other weekend in jail, to watch an autopsy performed on a wreck victim, to ride with an ambulance crew on emergency runs, and to work as a volunteer in a hospital emergency room.

Pigage was also ordered to share his experience with high school students at MADD lectures. This touched the Morrises' hearts and they went backstage to talk with him. Their frail sympathy evaporated when they smelled liquor on his breath. But . . .

Tommy Pigage still gets a lot of attention from the Morrises. Now they drive him to church twice a week and often set a place for him at their dinner table. Unable to find satisfaction through revenge, the couple recently decided to forgive Pigage and try to help him rebuild his life, along with rebuilding their own.

Frank and Elizabeth Morris came to realize that their whole lives were being distorted by their hatred. "We needed to forgive Tommy to save ourselves," they said. "I felt alcohol had already wiped out one very special life," she explained. "I didn't want to see it waste three more lives, too."

Frank and Elizabeth went to Tommy's cell over and over again until that young man finally, on one visit, wept and threw his arms around Frank, begging to be forgiven. They actually forgave him.

"We couldn't simply drop it at that point, though," the Morrises relate. "Maybe we would have felt a little better, but real forgiveness requires the second mile, to see what good we might be able to do for him." Tommy is, for all practical purposes, Frank and Elizabeth's adopted son today.

Not all forgiveness stories end so happily. But all who genuinely forgive do experience this kind of healing in their own hearts.

When you don't know quite how
to forgive someone,
Remember:
Forgiveness is something we *do,*
and we *can* do it—because God has
given us forgiveness through the cross.

---

*See how the masses of men
slowly lower themselves into nameless graves,
while here and there an unselfish soul
forgets himself into immortality.*
— *Ralph Waldo Emerson*

FOURTEEN

*In spite of all his problems, David knew deep joy
because of His relationship with God . . .*

He Went Out Singing

2 Samuel 22–23
1 Chronicles 29

rank is hardly 60, but he looks easily a decade older. He is sick, alone, and unemployed. Frank is my friend and I love him—but somewhere, years ago, he lost his way.

The other day as we lingered over coffee, Frank—in a rare moment of self-disclosure—slammed his fist on the table and bellowed, "Lynn, I'm bankrupt." Then punctuating his declaration with some choice expletives, he catalogued his fear and helplessness, "I'm bankrupt financially. I'm bankrupt physically. I'm bankrupt morally and emotionally. I'm also bankrupt spiritually.

217

But I don't want to do like so many old codgers do when they get sick and scared — turn to religion. That's a crock of . . . "

What *do* people think about when they see age creeping up and time running out? Do they dread the gathering darkness?

How do they go out? Crying? Tight-lipped, stoically waiting the inevitable? Do some go out screaming or pleading? Confessing? Cursing? I know some who have gone whispering good things. My grandfather was born in Sweden and reared in Wisconsin; then he homesteaded on the harsh plains of Saskatchewan back before the railroad was built. When he was near 80, and blind, he lived with us. I'll never forget Grandpa Eric standing out of the wind on the sunny side of a farm building, leaning on his handmade walking staff. He would stare long at nothing; then light would cross his sightless blue eyes, and he would whisper in his Scandinavian accent "Praise t' Lord."

Some even go out singing! Our friend David was one of these. His songs have been collected into the most lasting and widely sung hymnal of all the centuries. Extravagant celebrations decorated his declining days. Once, as aged David stood before an excited crowd,

> The king also rejoiced greatly . . . saying,
> "Praise be to you, O LORD,
> God of our father Israel,
> . . . we give you thanks,
> and praise your glorious name"
> > (1 Chronicles 29:9-13).

So all the people broke into a frenzy of praise: "They ate and drank with great joy in the presence of the LORD" (verse 22).

David went out singing. In fact,

These are the last words of David: "The oracle
of David son of Jesse,
. . . exalted by the Most High,
. . . anointed by the God of Jacob,
Israel's singer of songs" (2 Samuel 23:1).

Golden Years

Fascinating! Biographers profile David in many roles: shepherd, soldier, statesman, and dramatic sinner—but David styles himself "Israel's Singer of Songs." Question is: Why? How could David go out singing? The easy answer would be: He died at a good old age, having enjoyed life and having amassed a great deal of wealth and honor. Who wouldn't die happy if he lived a long time, had a lot of money, and was respected by a lot of people? But this is not the whole story.

Life was definitely not all peaches and cream for David, even in his golden years. David had traveled nearly eighty years over rough roads and in harsh times that left most men old at 30. His declining days were not simple either. In many respects, he was a weary, troubled, old man.

Surely he didn't spend his afternoons in the sun with no regrets. Remember, the same spirit which dreamed of a temple, trained a choir, and from his deathbed equipped his successor also lusted for the blood of Shimei to satisfy an old grudge. Old age found David still tortured by inner turmoil. He was also sick and cold and sexually impotent.

When King David was old and well advanced in years, he could not keep warm even when they put covers over him. So his servants . . . found Abishag . . . and brought her to the king. The girl . . . took care of the king . . . but the king had no intimate relations with her"

(1 Kings 1:1-4).

Ill health in old age is not glamorous!

Besides, trouble complicated David's life till the last days. Even while lying physically spent on his deathbed, David was forced to squash an attempted coup, as Adonijah, his spoiled son, tried an end-run around Solomon to seize the throne. How then, indeed, could David—old, sick, impotent, internally tortured and externally troubled—leave this world in celebration and song?

Tuning In

At a traffic light I witnessed a most amusing sight in the car beside me. An elderly gentleman was bobbing, slapping the dash in rhythm, and singing at the top of his lungs. When he spotted me watching him, rather than looking embarrassed, he grinned, then grabbed a card and held it up to the window to display the call letters of a local radio station. I punched that button on my radio, and in a few seconds I, too, was bobbing, slapping the dash, and singing at the top of my lungs. Until I was tuned in to his frequency, I did not hear his song, so could not know what made him sing!

Into what frequency was David tuned? What song did he hear that allowed him to go out singing?

David heard a song of *wonder*. He sang because he knew God was firmly in charge. God was not merely another component to a self-centered life in order to upgrade its quality. Rather, for David, God was the center of everything that matters—the one constant to which all life must adjust or die. For him, God was not merely to be included or explained, but to be hallowed, worshiped and obeyed. Listen to some of his praise to a transcended God:

> Yours, O LORD, is the greatness and the power
> and the glory and the majesty and the splendor
>   (1 Chronicles 29:11).

Far from seeing God as a benign old grandfather waiting eagerly to spoil all His children, David trembled before a holy and sovereign majesty.

> Who am I, O Sovereign LORD . . . that you have
> brought me this far? (2 Samuel 7:18)

The expression, "O Sovereign Lord" stands at the center of David's vocabulary. David repeats this phrase no less than seven times in ten verses.

> What more can David say to you? For you know
> your servant, O Sovereign LORD . . . How great
> you are, O Sovereign LORD! (2 Samuel 7:20-22)

David was overawed that such a God could care for him. Green pastures. Still water. Renewal. Guidance. The personal care of such an awesome sovereign enabled David to go out singing:

> Even though I walk
> through the valley of the shadow of death,
> . . . you are with me (Psalm 23:4).

Righteous and Blameless

David also shouted a song of *gratitude*. He sang because he knew he was forgiven, even of *his* earth-shattering sins. David, like my friend Frank, could have seen himself as bankrupt; instead he saw himself blameless. On his own, every person is bankrupt: "All have sinned and fall short of the glory of God" (Romans 3:23). David, however, made a strange boast:

> The LORD has dealt with me according to my
>   righteousness . . .
> For I have kept the ways of the LORD;
>   I have not done evil by turning from my God
>   (2 Samuel 22:21,22).

David, how can you say this? Are you not the same David who lied to the priests at Nob, saving your own skin but causing a whole town to be slaughtered? Was it not you, David, who committed adultery with the wife of a loyal friend? How can you speak of your "righteousness," David—you who treacherously murdered Uriah to cover your own stupidity?

Nevertheless, David continues:

> I have been blameless before him
>   and have kept myself from sin.
> The LORD has rewarded me according to my
>   righteousness (2 Samuel 22:24,25a).

David, are you speaking in relative terms, suggesting that since you did not turn away from God to idols, you are "relatively blameless"? Or are you singing a song of gratitude because you know you are forgiven?

David, I interrupted you in mid-sentence. Please finish the last line and answer my question.

> . . . according to my cleanness *in his sight"*
>   (verse 25b).

Blameless in God's sight. David is not boasting of his own virtues, but describing how God sees him. David knew God saw him as blameless, so as he moved into the valley of the shadow he went out singing, "Blessed is he whose transgressions are forgiven, whose sins are covered" (Psalm 32:1).

Without hearing this song, how does a person go out?

Fulfilled

Another note in David's song is *fulfillment*. He sang because he knew he had been used of God:

> When David had served God's purpose in his own generation, he fell asleep; he was buried with his fathers (Acts 13:36).

Ralph Waldo Emerson said: "See how the masses of men lower themselves into nameless graves, while here and there a selfless soul forgets himself into immortality."

David is definitely one of the immortals. His life, stated simply, was: "Never idols; always God." He pulled together one nation, with idols banished and with the ark resting at the center of Mt. Zion, while his songs rang, not only throughout that land, but throughout history.

Across the centuries, God's purposes for David have been clear. He foretold a coming Savior and became the central link in the chain from Adam to Jesus, the "Son of David." David's throne foreshadowed God's throne and shaped the vocabulary with which the kingdom of God would for all time be discussed.

As David "sleeps with his fathers," one can almost see him smile in his sleep. He went out singing the full rich baritone of fulfillment, knowing he had served God's purposes.

Few feel this way in their late years. The opposite is far more common.

> There are a lot of men who creep
> into the world to eat and sleep,
> and know no reason why they're born
> save only to consume the corn,
> devour the cattle, bread and fish,
> and leave behind an empty dish;
> and if their tombstones, when they die,
> were not to flatter or to lie,
> there's nothing better can be said
> than that they've eaten up their bread,
> drunk up their drink, and gone to bed!
> —Author unknown[1]

We sing our saddest songs longest if we live and die without a sense of purpose. What are you for? Forks are for eating. Hoes are for hoeing. Are human beings for nothing but to wander the earth a few years, then stagger off life's highway, and die like dogs in a ditch? This is obscene—but it is how the masses go out. It is why my friend Frank pounds his fist on the table. For what purpose are you passing through this world? How will you go out?

Hope

David's song also rang with *hope*. He sang because he knew that the relationship most important to him would not end at death. At the end we lose everything most of us value: fortune, friends, family and freedom.

Millions who search a lifetime for fortune, in the final analysis ride only to oblivion in the "back of a black limousine." Friends enrich life, too, but they can betray us or abandon us, and we will most likely move off and leave each other. All of my life I have been saying goodbye to someone I didn't think I could live without.

What could matter more than family? But families fall apart. Divorce, death, dissension — all shatter families. Children move away from parents, make their own lives, and at least partially forget. Parents are left alone. I know. Our baby left home this year.

When these are all gone, do we still have freedom? Paralysis and illness can imprison us in a room or a wheel chair. Totalitarianism or incarceration can rob us of all options. Death will finally seal us in a hole six by six by two.

> Death and decay and passing away
> are written on the winds of time.

A Constant Relationship

Only our relationship with God is unaffected by any change or circumstance, even by physical death. David knew this, and the one constant across all of his turbulent life was his relationship with God. His dominant lifelong search was for communion with Yahweh. In the dark days of struggle he pleaded:

> Hear my cry, O God . . .
> From the ends of the earth I call to you,
>   I call as my heart grows faint;
>   lead me to the rock that is higher than I
> (Psalm 61:1,2).

The central wailing cry of a heart which longs for God becomes the melody of David's song. Even when he was on the run, alone in the desert, his throat aching for water, David sang of a more urgent thirst:

> O God, you are my God,
>   earnestly I seek you;
> my soul thirsts for you,
>   my body longs for you,
> in a dry and weary land
>   where there is no water (Psalm 63:1).

We said earlier that the relationship most important to David would be unaffected by physical death. This is not completely true, because death will, in fact, improve this relationship.

We are forever destined, here on earth, to a certain degree of loneliness and unfulfillment. Our mortality stands in the way of complete intimacy with God. But David knew this veil would be lifted at last. He said, "My son cannot come to me, but I can go to him" (see 2 Samuel 12:23). Here we catch one of the few Old Testament glimpses into life beyond the grave.

Hope triggers the grand finale. If our final days bring us nearer life's highest priority, we do have something to sing about. So David could go out quietly humming his song of hope.

A Contrast

In the span of one week recently, I spent several intense hours, first, with my "bankrupt" friend Frank, then later with my 84-year-old father. The stark contrast haunts my dreams.

Frank is alone. He is unable to work. He is broke. He is aging, sick, and dying. Frank is frightened.

Yes, Frank is profoundly bankrupt. He pounds his fist on the table.

Dad is 84. When he leaves this world, no one will lose an enemy. He has been poor all of his life because he has always given away most of what he had. For Dad *relationships* have always elbowed his *possessions* to the periphery. Parkinson's disease took Mom last spring. First, her speech slurred, then she could not walk well or swallow easily. Then I noticed as we talked on the phone, the receiver kept sliding from her ear. Dad cared for her, hand and foot, twenty-four hours a day. He rarely slept more than an hour at a time. Although he was tired, he still enjoyed life. Finally, he could care for her no longer, so her last months passed in a rest home.

Dad is the happiest man I ever knew. He laughs a lot, loves a good joke or an old story. He writes poetry. A bundle of his poems overflows one of my file drawers. There are no sad songs among them, and these days he writes mostly about heaven.

Life is precious to him, but he has absolutely no fear of death. A good many of his treasures are already "over there." The last time I spent a couple of days with my dad, we sang a lot. He sang to Mom at the rest home that last year, too. Dad does not pound his fist on the table.

Dad is on his way out, and as he goes, he goes out singing.

Our world is full of songs sung at a feverish tempo, amplified too loudly, with lyrics that hold no hope. Such a cacophony of sound and kaleidoscope of motion swirls around us that, even if we should be tuned to the proper frequency, the song of David would almost be drowned out.

Almost. But what is that sound I hear?

A song of *worship* to a loving sovereign.

Gratitude for *forgiveness*.

Fulfillment because life serves God's purpose.

Hope enhanced by physical death. Such are the strains heard by David. Tuned in to this frequency, I, too, can go out singing!

So can you!

When all the problems of your life
overwhelm you,
Remember:
Your song can well up from a deep sense of
purpose and relationship with God.

---

*The heart is deceitful above all things
and beyond cure.
Who can understand it?*
—Jeremiah 17:9

*David sometimes doesn't understand himself,
but he becomes "every man" to let us know
God is **for** every man . . .*

On
Through
the Fog

Jeremiah 17:9

ed stepped cautiously into the noisy restaurant. Glancing right and left, he slipped into my booth, shoved his elbows nearer to my side of the table and mumbled, "I don't know what's wrong with me. Really, I want to be God's person—I think. But sometimes I don't want to. Often at church I swear I'll never be anything but Christian again. Then comes Monday. Back on the job

I not only forget how I felt Sunday, I don't even *want* that any more. Why, just yesterday I took the communion wine, and the next minute I found myself fantasizing about the woman across the aisle. Will I ever know integrity? Sometimes I wonder if there is any hope for a guy like me. I don't know if I have the heart to go on."

I hear you, Ted. I often wonder about this myself. I think King David did, too.

From the opening lines of this book we have followed his zigzag course between sunlight and shadow. The boy who risked his young life confronting Goliath is the man who lied to save his own skin, inviting the slaughter of a whole village. He wrote psalms, and he murdered his friend. He was both an adulterer and choirmaster. He defected to the Philistine army yet danced in an ecstasy of praise to God. He repeatedly forgave Saul but carried his grudge against Shimei to the grave. The same David who ignored good advice and triggered the death of seventy thousand innocent people is the man who gently carried the ark of God to holy Mount Moriah. His life swung like a pendulum between the pit and the pinnacle. Who could possibly have a more convoluted and confused heart than our old friend David?

Why David?

These thoughts bring us full circle from the beginning of this book. We can't help asking in the closing lines: Why does God place this rascal in such an imposing position? What earned David more lines of print than any other biblical figure? Why did the Almighty appoint David king of a chosen people, enable him to write The Song Book for the Centuries, and actually select him to *prefigure Christ*? Why?

The strange fact is that God did not single David out for special attention. David is not even the object of his story. We are. The Scripture does not include the story of David so we will admire David, but it's there so we can know God. Rather than searching the saga for some special virtue which qualified David for honor, we are better served to watch for windows into God's nature and bridges between us and Him.

My friend Ted needs such a bridge. Ted does not understand himself, nor did David. This is precisely why most people seem to connect with David so easily. I can't seem to identify with some biblical personalities. Take Paul, for example. While I respect him, Paul seems entirely too religious for my blood. I can't picture myself sitting down across the table for a cup of coffee with the man. Or how about Jeremiah? He scares the daylights out of me. Somehow this thundering prophet doesn't look like a fun fishing partner.

On the other hand, David strikes home. Ah, he is my man. His earthiness overlaps my own and puts me at ease. I can comfortably sit down at the table with David, maybe join in his conversation with God, maybe even find the heart to go on. You, too, right? David becomes every man in order to let us know that God is *for* every man.

The Heart

David also opens windows to the heart of the Almighty. David definitely was a bad actor. Yet God accepted him, warts and all. God was not put off by David's mistakes or impressed by his accomplishments.

"Man looks on the outward appearance," said Adonai in a thousand ways, "but I look on the *heart.*" He heard David say, "My *heart* is fixed [on you], O God" (Psal 57:7, KJV). When David finally confronted his own runaway pride, his *heart* attacked him. Crushed under guilt David cried out, "Create in me a clean *heart*, O God" (Psalm 51:10, KJV). God even affirmed David's temple dreams: "You did well to have this in your *heart*" (2 Chronicles 6:8).

Across nineteen years as minister of a relatively large church in a small city I have come to know the worst things about some of the "best people in town" and some amazing acts of courage and kindness by "the town's worst." I no longer classify people as good and bad.

Yet nearly every day I talk with people who are counting themselves out, like my friend Ted in the restaurant. Unable to live out consistently what they know is right, they give up on themselves and lose the heart to go on. God doesn't give up so easily. He is far more interested in where our roads are headed than in the speed we travel or the distance we have come. The bent of our hearts is what matters with Him.

 ## The Deceitful Heart

Wonderful, hopeful news!

But here comes the kicker. This you won't like to read. "The heart is deceitful above all things and beyond cure. Who can understand it?" (Jeremiah 17:9)

Mull over those concepts again, carefully: Deceptive. Cannot be cured. Cannot be fathomed. This mystery drove the apostle Paul to recite his uneasy frustration, "I do not understand what I do. For what I want to do I do not do, but what I hate I do" (Romans 7:15). He must have been reading my mail. Paul definitely resonates with another of my friends, Hal.

Hal called late one night. "God has blessed my business beyond anything I had dreamed. What can I say? I'm rich, okay? And some people say I'm powerful. And man, I love to give money to good causes. But what bothers me is that I am hooked on the power trip I get from giving. On one hand, I really get high about my reputation as a generous man who has done well, and I love to be in control. On the other hand, I really think I love God and care about people and do want to see the kingdom expand. But when I put the ink on my checks, I often get this ego rush. And I wonder which motives are the real ones, love or ego. How can I know?"

Jeremiah said, "The heart is so deceitful that we will never be able to understand it." We don't want to believe this, however. We would rather believe that most people, given sufficient information and proper encouragement, will do the right thing. We take pride in our independent self-management and we attempt to bolster it in all sorts of ways. One way is to cram our skulls with data, thinking if we just learn the right stuff our hearts will heal. The Word of God definitely is "living and active . . . [and] it judges the thoughts and attitudes of the heart" (Hebrews 4:12). It strips us naked before a God who peers into our souls. This frightens us, disturbs us, pains us. Consequently, sometimes we find it safer to study the Bible solely for information so that we wind up gathering Bible knowledge to avoid confrontation with God rather than using it as a means of opening our hearts to Him.

Some of us attempt to iron the wrinkles out of our souls by introspection. My friend Randal discovered the futility of this approach. Randal's ministry became paralyzed by obsessive self-examination. Over the long-distance wires he confided, "If I could only understand more about myself, I would know how to manage myself. I feel God has called me to this ministry, but I am also painfully aware that some cheap motives drive me as well. I run on attention and respect and I eat up the affirmation. While standing in front of an audience teaching the Word of God, I have actually caught myself thinking, 'Boy, it's nice to have all this power, hundreds of people hanging on every word.'

"But in more sober moments I definitely want to glorify God and I do want to see broken people cared for and lost people saved. Which is the real me? Trying to sort through my motives has only confused and paralyzed me. I am totally preoccupied with myself. I have been staring at my own navel so long I have lost my balance."

To recover equilibrium Randal had to look outside himself—set his eyes on the horizon. God took care of his navel. Analysis is not the answer.

Other people look for a set formula. Backed against the wall by the mystery of their own motives, they would love to get their hands on a mechanism which clearly distinguishes Dr. Jekyl from Mr. Hyde.

Confusion

A bright and warm lady came to my office in search of this formula. Doris had cheated on her husband. The affair was over several years back and her husband, Alan, never knew. Now their marriage is healthy and their high school children love and respect their parents. Alan has always trusted Doris implicitly, but she has led counselor after counselor through her litany of options. "Even though I believe God has forgiven me, I fear I will always be living a lie if I do not confess to Alan and clear the deck. On the other hand," Doris agonizes, "confessing might actually do more harm than good. Why hurt Alan and the kids now that all this is behind me? Or am I just using this 'hurt' thing as an excuse for not facing the music?"

Doris wrestles on, "Part of me wonders if I want to confess simply to make myself feel better and to ease the guilt. Another part of me wonders if it is the other way around; that I have chosen not to confess in order to avoid pain. I don't know what's right to do because I'm not sure about my motives."

Doris still hasn't found the formula. No question about it. The heart definitely is confusing.

We even try to run from our confusion. We plunge into a thousand activities, moving fast and hoping the wind will roar loud enough in our ears to drown out the questioning voices inside us. David reflects:

> Where can I go from your Spirit?
> Where can I flee from your presence?
> If I go up to the heavens, you are there;
>   if I make my bed in the depths, you are there
>   (Psalm 139:7,8).

We run but we cannot hide. Eventually we must confront the dark mystery of our confused hearts.

God often leaves us with paradox and ambiguity. Of course we are uncomfortable with this. We want things to be clear cut and all our heroes to wear white hats. When life comes down into the gray zones, we are disappointed and disillusioned, thinking something is wrong with us—or with God. Cynicism may settle in. Or we may restlessly pursue resolution of our ambiguities.

🜲 The Truth

Yet one fundamental truth stands firmly in our way: Sin has knocked our universe out of kilter. Nothing works. Things don't get better. Nothing gets permanently fixed. Our hearts don't make sense. Because we are immortals trapped in mortality, nothing can totally fulfill us here. The sooner we accept these facts the better off we will be. Hope comes only after we acknowledge our desperate need for God.

Our old friend David was finally driven to this realization. That is why he so boldly prayed:

Search me, O God, and know my *heart*;
  test me and know my anxious thoughts.
See if there is any offensive way in me,
  and lead me in the way everlasting
          (Psalm 139:23,24).

He knew that we cannot manage ourselves and that only God understands our mixed hearts well enough to sort the gold from the dross. Self-understanding, self-management and self-justification all fall silent before the almighty and sovereign God. He alone understands the thoughts and intents of our hearts. Only He can lead us in paths of righteousness.

My friend Landon Saunders tells about a visit with his mother during her advanced years. She had come from humble surroundings and married young. Yet with little education and through extremely tough circumstances, she had hung in and cheerfully reared her family.

"How were you able to keep at it?" Landon queried.

She thought a bit, then replied, "Well, each morning, I just decided to get up and go on."

David's Determination

Landon's mother understood that when we cannot unravel the mysteries of the heart, we often must simply determine to get up and go on. David did. His resolute intentionality jumps out at us in the end of the twenty-third psalm. David begins the psalm addressing fellow human beings. Then a strange thing happens in the middle of it. As if caught up in heavenly reverie, he suddenly switches audiences and we hear him talking, not to us, but to God. Praise rises to a crescendo, driving toward the last determined line:

> I will dwell in the house of the LORD forever
> (Psalm 23:6*b*).

David may have been a shuffling old man, with gray head, lined face, and tears flooding his watery eyes, but he was never broken. Never. Oh, yes, he fully comprehended the depths of his own sin and accepted complete responsibility for it. His failures would have killed a lesser man.

Yet in spite of the awfulness of his life, David still declared, "I am not leaving the house of the Lord." He didn't say, "I hope that one day I will get to dwell in the house of the Lord." He said, "*I will dwell!*" Our man David was stubborn. "I will not turn loose. I may mark up the walls; I may spill on the rug and break up the furniture; but I ain't leavin'. I will stay—forever. No matter how many mistakes I make or sins I commit, I will continually come back to God, leave my blunders with Him, and go on."

Our Misery and God's Mercy

We are all marred. If everyone in the world rolled down a hill together, we would all go "thump-thump-thump." Like my friends Ted, Hal and Doris, and our friend David, we, too, are impaired by sin, and we seldom totally understand our own motives. Our contradictory desires confuse us and demoralize us. Our weakness overwhelms us, till we feel that we really don't belong with righteous people or that we're losing the heart to go on.

These are the times to remember that God is the center of love. Any direction we move away from God is a move farther into misery. God does not stand remote and aloof. Salvation is not dangled beyond the reach of ordinary people. God can be trusted to sort out all the elements of our tangled souls.

He is patient with you, not wanting anyone to perish, but everyone to come to repentance
                        (2 Peter 3:9).

By grace you have been saved, through faith— and this not from yourselves, it is the gift of God (Ephesians 2:8,9).

This hope lifts us up to go on, to determine that we will stay in the house of the Lord. We don't belong anywhere else, because we are His.

The Lord is our shepherd, still. With Him, twentieth-century urbanites want for nothing. He leads high-tech people in paths of righteousness. Our cup can overflow. His goodness and mercy travel our freeways, too. A thousand years before Christ, David told us so.

When our son Christopher was four, Baskin-Robbins ice cream rated high on his good-time list. Wednesday ice-cream trips were out because I had a standing obligation at work. However, one Wednesday a preannounced cancellation freed me to promise Chris a trip to Baskin-Robbins. As Murphy's law would have it, whatever can go wrong, will — and at the last minute another meeting was called.

As I rolled into the driveway at 11:30 P.M., Chris met me in his pajamas, lower lip protruding and dry salt trailing down his cheeks.

"Dad, you lied to me."

"I wouldn't lie to you, son. There wasn't supposed to have been a meeting."

"But, Dad, you teach us kids that when you say different from what is, it's a lie; and you said different from what is."

Down on my knees, eye to eye with him, I apologized. "Son, I thought it was true, but really it wasn't. I'm sorry. Could you forgive me?"

"Aw, that's okay, Dad; good people have to lie all the time."

Shock! My eyes were riveted to his. "What do you mean, son?"

"Well, Dad, the policemen on TV lie to the bad guys to protect the good guys."

"Surely a Christian policeman could find another way. God doesn't want his people to lie."

"No, Dad, in Sunday school, we studied about Rahab, the harlot lady. She hid God's good guys and lied to the bad guys. *God blessed her for that lie*, Dad."

I threw in the towel. "Maybe we could use some Gatorade."

My golden-haired son with his wide, sky-blue eyes retaught me something I cannot afford to forget. We can't know all the answers, and when we discover mystifying contradictions in our own hearts, this does not automatically mean our relationship with God has gone down the tubes.

"Son," I said, "I don't know the answer. But this is a good time to learn something very important. As we walk with Jesus, we won't understand everything along the way; sometimes we won't even understand ourselves and why we do what we do. But if we just hold on to His hand, in the end everything will be all right."

Chris and I hugged and whisper-sang a favorite family song:

> My Lord knows the way
> Through the wilderness.
> All I have to do is follow . . .
> Follow . . . follow.

Because he was a man after God's own heart, David never gave up on his relationship with God. This is precisely what is godlike about David's heart.

God did not give up on His relationship with David, either. Nor does He give up on us. No matter where we are, or what we have done, or where things appear to be headed at this point in life, He is calling us on. All we have to do is follow.

> Do you despair because, like David,
> you sometimes bounce back and forth
> between spirituality and worldliness?
> **Remember:**
> You don't need to give up;
> your eternal home is assured
> in the house of the Lord forever.

Farewell, friend David. Thank you.
You have helped me.
And thank you, Adonai.
I cannot live without You.
Along with Winston Churchill, I will never,
never, never give up. I will intentionally and
resolutely "dwell in the house of the LORD."

I have found enough heart to go on — forever.

Reference Notes

Chapter 1   Because He Had the Heart

1. Tony Compolo, *Success Fantasy* (Wheaton, IL: Victor Books, 1973), p. 6.
2. Henri Nouwen, *The Way of the Heart* (New York: Ballantine Bks., 1981) pp. 13-14.
3. Ruth Harms Calkin, *Tell Me Again, Lord, I Forget* (Elgin, IL: David C. Cook Publishing Co., 1974), p. 37.

Chapter 6   God of Death and God of Dancing

1. R. C. Sproul, *The Holiness of God* (Wheaton, IL: Tyndale House Publishers, Inc., 1985), p. 147.

Chapter 8   Taking the Big Hit

1. Deitrich Bonhoeffer, *Temptation* (New York: Macmillan Company, 1955), p. 116.
2. Ibid, p. 117.
3. Don Francisco, "I Don't Care Where You've Been Sleeping," from the album *Live Concert* (Benson, Zondervan Music Group, 1978). Used by permission.

Chapter 9   Caring Enough to Confront

1. Charles Swindoll, "Riding Out the Storm," tape #320, *The Shepherd's Voice,* 1978.

Chapter 10   Families in the Fast Lane

1. "What Entertainers Are Doing to Your Kids," *U. S. News & World Report* (October 28, 1985), pp. 46-49.
2. National Gallup Youth Survey. Reprinted from the *TAD Newsletter*, Jackson, TN (December 1984).
3. Willard and Marguerite Beecher, *Parents on the Run* (Marina Del Rey, CA: DeVorss, 1983), pp. 30-31.
4. *Newsweek* 104:50 (December 10, 1985).
5. Roger Rosenblatt, "The Freedom of the Damned," *Time* (October 6, 1986).
6. Will Allen Dromcoole, "The Bridgebuilder," in *Best Loved Poems of the American People,* selected by Hazel Fellman (Garden City, NY: Doubleday & Co., Inc., 1936).

Chapter 11   When a Father's Heart Is Breaking

1. "What Entertainers Are Doing to Your Kids," *U. S. News & World Report* (October 28, 1985), pp. 46-49. Also *Communique: Texans' War on Drugs,* Austin, Texas, from the National Gallup Youth Survey.
2. John White, *Parents in Pain* (Downers Grove, IL: InterVarsity Press, 1979), p. 106.

Chapter 12   Aging With Class

1. Henri Nouwen and Walter J. Gaffney, *Aging: The Fulfillment of Life* (Garden City, NY: Doubleday & Co., Inc., 1974), p. 71.

Chapter 14   He Went Out Singing

1. Quoted by J. Wallace Hamilton, *Horns and Halos in Human Nature* (Old Tappan, NJ: Fleming H. Revell Co., 1950), p. 120.

Life-Changing Reading

Kathy — Peggy Runyon
1   393-0800
         758-8400